Evelyn Waugh's Officers, Gentlemen, and Rogues
The Fact behind His Fiction

Gene D. Phillips

Evelyn Waugh's
Officers, Gentlemen, and Rogues
The Fact behind His Fiction

 Nelson-Hall Chicago

Copyright © 1975 by Gene D. Phillips

All rights reserved. No part of this book may be reproduced
in any form without permission in writing from the publisher,
except by a reviewer who wishes to quote brief passages in
connection with a review written for broadcast or for inclusion
in a magazine or newspaper. For information address Nelson-Hall
Inc., 325 W. Jackson Boulevard, Chicago, Illinois   60606.

Manufactured in the United States of America.

Library of Congress Cataloging in Publication Data

Phillips, Gene D
    Evelyn Waugh's officers, gentlemen, and rogues.

    Bibliography: p.
    Includes index.
    1. Waugh, Evelyn, 1903-1966.   I. Title.
PR6045.A97Z75   823'.9'12   75-26546
ISBN 0-88229-172-6

For
My Father and Mother

The significance of the Evelyn Waugh diaries is to show
that the world of Evelyn Waugh's novels did, in fact, exist.

Auberon Waugh
New York Times Magazine

Contents

Preface

"Every writer borrows what he needs from himself," the American novelist Saul Bellow once said to me. Evelyn Waugh, in a similar vein, once wrote: "The novelist does not come to his desk devoid of experience and memory. His raw material is compounded of all he has seen and done."[1]

For years readers and critics alike have speculated about the extent to which Evelyn Waugh's personal life and opinions found their way into his novels. Clues were scattered in his travel books, which are, to some degree, autobiographical studies; his unfinished autobiography, *A Little Learning*, which ends just as its subject reaches the threshold of his writing career; the brief autobiographical prefaces he wrote for the Second Uniform Edition of his works, published a few years before his death in 1966; the essays he published throughout his life, frequently about topics that also served as subjects for his fiction; and his semi-autobiographical novel *The Ordeal of Gilbert Pinfold*, Waugh's fictionalized portrait of himself in middle life.

Now Waugh's private diary, made public in 1973, reveals that his fiction contains more of the things he did and the people he knew than any critic had imagined. Waugh's own opinion of his diary was not high. The manuscript of his autobiography contains this passage, which he later deleted: "Only in adolescence, during my last years at school and again from June, 1924, to September, 1926, when I was, it seemed, stagnating, did I write a diary with any candor and completeness. . . . I lack the art and ambition of the diarist and must resort to a memory which, alas, has proved more retentive of pain than pleasure."[2]

However, Waugh's diary has proved to be rich in information about his life and ideas, bringing into focus all the suggestions gleaned from other sources as to how Waugh utilized his experiences as raw material for his novels, demonstrating how much fact underlies an author's fiction. Indeed, the publication of Waugh's diary is one of the great literary events of the century. Virginia Woolf is the only other major twentieth-century English novelist to have left such a complete personal record. Waugh's diary entries begin when he was twelve and end just before his death.

After his death Waugh's widow, Laura, sent the diary to the University of Texas, which had become the recipient of her husband's entire library. Then, in 1972, the Waugh family granted permission for publication of the diary in the *London Observer*. It appeared in spring, 1973, as the longest serial ever undertaken by that journal. Now at last the critic of Waugh's work had a guidepost by which he could ascertain precisely how Waugh went about drawing on his own life to create his fictional world. As I will show, Waugh was able to transmute into fiction whatever experiences life offered him. His divorce from his first wife becomes the basis for *A Handful of Dust;* his conversion to Catholicism is at the heart of *Brideshead Revisited;* and his years of war service give a vital sense of reality to his trilogy,*Sword of Honor.*

The diary also enables us to see how Waugh's personal vision, as expressed in his fiction, developed throughout his lifetime. Literary critics often speak of the *persona* of a novelist, a term which refers to the impression one gets of an author's personal vision by reading his works. The way in which a novelist distributes the reader's sympathy for various characters indicates his own view of them. From the values the author has thus incorporated into the story, the reader can build an image of the author's *persona* – the sum of the novelist's vision, the totality of the attitudes and opinions implied in his fiction to be his own.

With the help of Waugh's diary, as well as his other autobiographical and nonfiction writings, the reader can now grasp just how close the personal vision of Waugh the novelist was to that of Waugh the man. Waugh saw modern man as drifting further and further from the traditional values of western civilization, concretely embodied for him in his religious faith and in his loyalty to his country. He sought to enshrine these values in his fiction. "The writer's only service to the disintegrated society of today," he once explained, "is to create little independent systems of order of his own" ("Fan-fare," *Life*, 8 April 1946).

To gain further insights into Waugh's life and work I corresponded with his brother Alec, who served as consultant to the publishers of the diary, and interviewed his widow and several other members of the Waugh family (Teresa, Auberon, Harriet, and Septimus) as well as acquaintances including his lifelong friend Rev. Martin D'Arcy, S.J. What they told me gave me a greater understanding of the material about Waugh's life and work than I could have gotten simply from his writings.

Because Waugh's diary had been sent to the University of Texas after his death, none of the Waugh family had read it at the time the *London Observer Magazine* requested permission to serialize it. There has been some speculation as to whether his family would have allowed publication had they read it beforehand. But as Waugh's eldest son, Auberon, writes in the *New York Times Magazine* (7 October 1973), the diary is a significant work because it shows "that the world of Evelyn Waugh's novels did, in fact, exist." Auberon also points out that the diary was edited for publication by Michael Davie with great discretion. Waugh's oldest daughter, Teresa D'Arms, believes that the personal nature of her father's diary suggests he probably had not intended to publish it, although he would certainly have drawn on it extensively had he lived to finish his autobiography.[3]

My own opinion is that Waugh himself very likely would not have published his diary, if for no other reason than that it would make the task of future literary critics too easy! Waugh elaborated upon his feelings about providing material for scholarly investigation of his novels in *The Ordeal of Gilbert Pinfold*. Concerning the novels of Mr. Pinfold (a character Waugh admits was based largely on himself), he writes:

> Foreign students often chose them as the subject of theses, but those who sought to detect cosmic significance in Mr. Pinfold's work, to relate it to fashions in philosophy, social predicaments or psychological tensions, were baffled by his frank, curt replies to questionnaires; their fellows in the English Literature School who chose more egotistical writers often found their theses more than half composed for them. . . . He regarded his books as objects which he had made, things quite external to himself to be used and judged by others.[4]

Nonetheless, whether or not one agrees with Graham Greene's remark in the *London Times* (15 April 1966) that "Evelyn Waugh was the greatest novelist of my generation," there is no doubt that Waugh's fiction deserves and repays critical analysis. The primary purpose of this study of Waugh is to show how much of his personal experience and world view made their way into his fiction.

Since Waugh's personal life and attitudes influenced his work throughout his life, I shall begin by sketching his early years. I shall show how he began developing the keen eye of a novelist who was to base dozens of his characters on people he knew and how he first encountered those religious conflicts that were to dog his heroes. The reader who accompanies me in this investigation may increase his enjoyment of those entertaining, thought-provoking novels created by one of the best fiction writers of our age.

Acknowledgments

Grateful acknowledgment is made to:

The late Laura Waugh, most especially, who kindly invited me to the Waugh home in Somerset, England, and who shared with me recollections of her husband's life and work.

The other members of Waugh's immediate family — Teresa, Auberon, Harriet, and Septimus — whom I was fortunate enough to be able to consult about this book.

Rev. Martin D'Arcy, S.J., and Rev. Thomas Corbishley, S.J., who recalled for me memories of their association with Evelyn Waugh, and Rev. Philip Caraman, S.J., who also knew Evelyn Waugh, for his valuable suggestions on how to proceed with this study.

Alec Waugh, Evelyn Waugh's brother; Christopher Sykes, Evelyn Waugh's official biographer; and those of Waugh's friends whom I was privileged to meet or correspond with during the preparation of this book.

Maryvonne Butcher of the *Tablet*, Ronald Brown of the Farm St. Library, and Phyllis Owen (all of London, England), and John Dowling of Boston, Massachusetts, all of whom provided me with vital research materials.

Acknowledgments

Mark Gerson, Evelyn Waugh's personal photographer, for permission to use the portrait of Waugh that appears in this book.

The staff (especially Judy Washburn) of the Cudahy Library of Loyola University of Chicago, and William Poplis, my research assistant.

Acknowledgment is also made for permission to quote from the works of Evelyn Waugh copyrighted as follows:

Chapman and Hall, London; and Little, Brown, Boston: *Decline and Fall* © 1928, 1956, 1962 by Evelyn Waugh. *Vile Bodies* © 1930, 1958, 1965 by Evelyn Waugh. *Black Mischief* © 1932, 1962 by Evelyn Waugh. *A Handful of Dust* © 1934, 1964 by Evelyn Waugh. *Mr. Loveday's Little Outing and Other Sad Stories* © 1936 by Evelyn Waugh. *Scoop* © 1938, 1964 by Evelyn Waugh. *Put Out More Flags* © 1942, 1966 by Evelyn Waugh. *Brideshead Revisited* © 1945, 1960 by Evelyn Waugh. *The Loved One* © 1948, 1965 by Evelyn Waugh. *Helena* © 1950, 1962 by Evelyn Waugh. *Men at Arms* © 1952, 1965 by Evelyn Waugh. *Love among the Ruins* © 1953, 1954 by Evelyn Waugh. *Officers and Gentlemen* © 1955, 1965 by Evelyn Waugh. *The Ordeal of Gilbert Pinfold* © 1957 by Evelyn Waugh. *Ronald Knox* © 1959 by Evelyn Waugh. *Tourist in Africa* © 1960 by Evelyn Waugh. *Unconditional Surrender* (American title: *The End of the Battle)* © 1961, 1965 by Evelyn Waugh. *Basil Seal Rides Again* © 1962, 1963 by Evelyn Waugh. *A Little Learning* © 1964 by Evelyn Waugh.

Duckworth, London; and Little, Brown, Boston: *Labels* (American title: *A Bachelor Abroad)* © 1930, 1947 by Evelyn Waugh.

Longmans, Greene, London; and Little, Brown, Boston: *Waugh in Abyssinia* © 1936, 1947 by Evelyn Waugh.

Doubleday, New York: "Come Inside" © 1949 by Evelyn Waugh, in *The Road to Damascus,* ed. John A. O'Brien.

Queen Anne Press, London: *The Holy Places* © 1952 by Evelyn Waugh.

Time-Life, Inc.: "Fan-fare" © 1946 by Evelyn Waugh.

Observer Magazine, London: *The Private Diaries of Evelyn Waugh* © 1973 by the Evelyn Waugh Estate.

Acknowledgments

Acknowledgment for permission to quote other works is made to:

The Viking Press, New York: Graham Greene, "The Redemption of Mr. Joyboy" © 1949, 1973 by Graham Greene; Julian Jebb, "Evelyn Waugh: An Interview," *Writers at Work* © 1967 by *Paris Review*.

Metheun, London: Andrew Rutherford, "Waugh's *Sword of Honor*" © 1968 by Andrew Rutherford.

Victor Gollancz, London: Christopher Sykes, "Waugh the Man," *Good Talk* © 1968 by Christopher Sykes.

1

Introduction: A Little Learning

Arthur Evelyn St. John Waugh was born on 28 October 1903. "I never liked the name," he confides in his autobiography, *A Little Learning*, "the first name after my father; the second from a whim of my mother's. . . . In America it is used only of girls and from time to time even in England it has caused confusion as to my sex." More than once a reception committee eagerly awaiting "Evelyn Waugh, English writer" greeted him with a bouquet of flowers intended for a lady novelist.[5]

The family into which Waugh was born had what he called in his essay "Come Inside" "a strong hereditary predisposition toward the Established Church. My family tree burgeons on every twig with Anglican Clergymen." "My father," Waugh says in the same essay, "was what was called a 'sound churchman'; that is to say, he attended church regularly and led an exemplary life." At the age of ten Evelyn showed his interest in things religious by composing "a long and tedious poem about Purgatory in the meter of *Hiawatha*" which was called "The World to Come"; he furthermore expressed his intention of becoming a clergyman, "to the dismay of my parents, who held a just estimate of my character."

Evelyn could not follow family tradition by attending Sherbourne because his brother Alec's satirical novel *The Loom of Youth* (1917), based on Alec's life there, had forced his father to choose another school for Evelyn. The novel more than hinted that homosexuality was practiced among the boys — something which everyone knew to be true of boys' boarding schools, Alec Waugh has said, but which no one before Alec had spoken or written about so candidly.

Evelyn's father, recognizing the lad's religious temperament, accordingly sent Evelyn to the school "which was reputed to have the strongest ecclesiastical bent." This was Lancing, a minor boarding school of pronounced Anglican traditions, where the students went to chapel twice daily and three times on Sunday. Evelyn Waugh did not find this excessive, however, until after he declared himself an agnostic. Concerning this period of religious doubt Waugh writes, "At the age of sixteen I formally notified the school chaplain that there was no God." Young Evelyn then inquired whether this religious position would disqualify him from his post as sacristan of the school chapel. He was genially assured that it was quite in order for a nonbeliever to act as sacristan. "The shallowness of my early piety," he concludes, "is shown by the ease with which I abandoned it." He continues:

> I have no doubt that I was a prig and a bore but I think that if I had been a Catholic boy in a Catholic school I should have found among its teaching orders someone patient enough to examine with me my callow presumption. Also, if I had been fortified by the sacraments, I should have valued my faith too highly to abandon it so capriciously. At my school I was quite correctly regarded as "going through a phase" normal to all clever boys, and left to find my own way home.[6]

Waugh records in his diary having gone for a long walk with another student one afternoon and thrashing out his religious difficulties with him. "It clears up one's ideas tremendously," he decided, "having to put them into words" (2 February 1920).

On a later walk with the same comrade (identified only as

"Luncher"), the seventeen-year-old Waugh learned that what his older brother Alec had written about boarding school homosexuality in *The Loom of Youth* was amply verified in his companion's admissions, which "revealed depths of lust and depravity for which I never gave him credit" (Easter 1921).

Evelyn went to Hertford College of Oxford University when he finished school, but his academic attainments fell far short of those of his father and brother, who had preceded him at Oxford. "From the first," he explains, "I regarded Oxford as a place to be inhabited and enjoyed for itself, not as the preparation for anywhere else." Some of the acquaintances he made at Oxford became lifelong friends; they included Graham Greene, Anthony Powell, Christopher Sykes, and Christopher Hollis, all of whom became writers. Others served as the basis for characters in Waugh's fiction. After all, "the novelist does not come to his desk devoid of experience and memory," he reminds readers of his autobiography. "His raw material is compounded of all he has seen and done." Thus Ambrose Silk of *Put Out More Flags* and Anthony Blanche of *Brideshead Revisited* were to a great extent drawn from Brian Howard, "an incorrigible homosexual" who had "dash and insolence, a gift of invective and repartee, . . . a kind of ferocity of elegance that belonged to the romantic era of a century before our own." The rogue Basil Seal in *Black Mischief* and other stories is a combination of Basil Murray, "a satanic young man," and Peter Rodd, "a man of action with his thoughts on the high seas and the desert."[7]

Waugh himself was not exemplary in his behavior during the years after Oxford, as he was the first to admit. From 1924 to 1928, when he published his first novel, *Decline and Fall*, he had no steady job and no prospects for a career: "I came down from Oxford without a degree, wanting to be a painter. My father settled my debts and I tried to become a painter. I failed, as I had neither the talent nor the application — I didn't have the moral qualities."[8]

The frustrated artist then became the frustrated novelist as

Waugh tried his hand at writing fiction. His earliest attempt had taken the form of a short story which he wrote at the age of seven years and one month. It was called "The Curse of the Horse Race" and ended with the strong moral: "I hope the story will be a leson [sic] never to bet."[9] While at school he had written a five-thousand-word novel about modern school life. Then he had embarked upon an Oxford novel called *The Temple at Thatch*, "which concerned an undergraduate who inherited a property of which nothing was left except an Eighteenth Century classical folly where he set up house and, I think, practiced black magic."

Waugh continued working on the novel during a shortlived career as prep-school teacher. He sent the first chapters to his friend Harold Acton, soliciting criticism but hoping for praise. Acton's reply was courteous but cool: "Too English for me. Too much nid-nodding over port." "I did not then, nor do I now, dispute his judgment," Waugh commented afterwards. "I took the exercise book in which the chapters were written and consigned it to the furnace of the school boiler."[10]

Waugh's tenure as prep-school master lasted two years, during which he taught at two private schools. The first was Arnold House, a small prep school in North Wales, the second a school near Aston Clinton for backward students. But aside from providing material for Waugh's first novel, *Decline and Fall*, his career as a teacher was a failure. He returned home penniless, to the great disappointment of his father. His twenty-first birthday passed without celebration.

Waugh's unfinished autobiography, *A Little Learning*, carries his life only to the year 1925, when his fortunes had reached their lowest ebb. Alec had tried to obtain for him a job as personal secretary to Proust's translator, C. K. Scott-Moncrieff. When the job failed to materialize, Evelyn found himself at the end of his tether. Once before, during his period of agnosticism at Lancing, he had noted in his diary thoughts of suicide: "I really think that if it weren't for my parents I should kill myself" (18 July

4

1921). Now his suicidal thoughts returned; and so, one night soon after he had lost hope of getting the secretarial position, "I went down alone to the beach with my thoughts full of death. I took off my clothes and began swimming out to sea."

Had he really intended to drown himself? "That certainly was in my mind and I left a note with my clothes, the quotation from Euripides about the sea which washes away all human ills. I went to the trouble of verifying it, accents and all, from the school text." He used a quotation from Euripedes' *Iphigenia in Tauris* which can be translated, "The sea washes away all the evils of men." "At my present age," Waugh concludes on the last page of his autobiography, "I cannot tell how much real despair and act of will, how much play-acting, prompted the excursion." At any rate, after being stung by several jellyfish, the would-be suicide returned to shore. "As earnest of my intent I had brought no towel. With some difficulty I dressed and tore into small pieces my pretentious classical tag, leaving them to the sea. . . . Then I climbed the sharp hill that led to all the years ahead."[11]

Among the things that lay immediately ahead of Waugh was the beginning of his career as a professional writer. In this brief introductory chapter I have shown Waugh taking his first steps toward that goal. While the fiction that he wrote as a student and later as a teacher did not prove worthy of publication, Waugh's experiences on both sides of the teacher's desk were about to lead to his first genuinely successful work of fiction: a novel about boarding-school life called *Decline and Fall*.

That Waugh was learning how to shape his personal experience into fiction is further underlined by the two books that followed *Decline and Fall* — *Vile Bodies*, which caricatured the social set in which he moved after he gave up teaching, and *Black Mischief*, the first of his novels to be based on his international travels. How Waugh began to absorb his life experiences as he encountered them, transforming them into the stuff of fiction, will become evident from a study of these first three novels.

2

Exile from Eden:
The Early Satires

Referring to his own literary output, Waugh once quipped, "I'm a very lazy man. My whole life's a vacation, occasionally interrupted by work." He described his method of composition as a combination of thinking first and then writing: "You know, you go out for a walk, get a thought, come back, alter a sentence. The thing goes along. About on the average each sentence is written certainly twice. All from longhand, of course, no dictating, no typewriting. Just push the words around and change them, you know."[12]

In his youth, Waugh was a whirlwind author. His early novels took six weeks apiece, including revision. He later slowed down perceptibly. By the time he wrote his trilogy of war novels, each novel was taking him a year, during which he worked off and on; during his concentrated work periods, two thousand words were "a good day's work." "One's memory gets so much worse," he explained late in his career. "I used to be able to hold the whole of a book in my head. Now if I take a walk whilst I am writing, I have to hurry back and make a correction, before I forget it."[13]

Teresa D'Arms recalls that her father did a great deal of revision in his later years: "I remember quite vividly his saying at the end of the day, when one of us asked how his writing had gone, 'I did an additional five hundred words or so today, but I redid much of what I wrote yesterday.'"

Waugh's failure in his first attempt to write a novel probably contributed to the despondency which led to his suicide attempt soon after he abandoned *The Temple at Thatch*. However, the mild but favorable reception given his life of Dante Gabriel Rossetti, which he wrote to support himself after he had lost his second teaching position, encouraged Waugh to try his hand at fiction once more.

Decline and Fall (1928)

In 1928, at the age of twenty-five, Waugh published *Decline and Fall*, based on his experiences as a school master. He first took the manuscript to Duckworth's, which had published the Rossetti volume; they turned it down flatly "on the odd grounds of its indelicacy," Waugh writes in his preface to the Second Uniform Edition of the novel (1962):

> I carried it down the street to Chapman and Hall. The Managing Director, my father, was abroad and was spared the embarrassment of a decision which was taken in his absence by a colleague, the late Mr. Ralph Straus. Mr. Straus read the manuscript carefully to see what could have shocked Duckworth's. He had a few suggestions which I accepted.

Mr. Straus thought it "more chaste," for instance, that the Llanabba station master should serve as procurer for his sister-in-law than for his sister. He also made some literary criticisms which Waugh found "less valuable. The result was a text differing slightly from the original manuscript." The 1962 edition restored the original text even though Mr. Straus's changes were, in Waugh's own words, "negligible."[14]

In a further effort to allay the misgivings of Chapman and Hall, the firm that was to remain Waugh's London publisher throughout his career. Waugh prefixed an "Author's Note" to the 1928 edition of *Decline and Fall:*

> I hope that my publishers are wrong when they say that this is a shocking novelette. I did not mean it to be when I wrote it, and I do not believe that anyone with a sense of humor will find it so. Still less is it a book with a purpose. I hope that somewhere a school like Llanabba may exist, and a staff like Dr. Fagan's, but it has never been my good fortune to come across them. . . . Please bear in mind throughout that IT IS MEANT TO BE FUNNY.

Waugh's assertion that *Decline and Fall* was not based on his real-life experiences as a teacher must have been made in order to avoid possible libel suits by some of the people he caricatures in the novel, for his diaries and autobiography prove quite the contrary. The most spectacular example is the character of the infamous Captain Grimes, for which Waugh's fellow teacher served as source. In fact Waugh later pointed to Grimes as a prime example of a fictional character based on a real person. In a *Life* magazine essay entitled "Fan-fare" he wrote of his works:

> All the major characters are the result of numberless diverse observations fusing in the imagination into a single whole. My problem has been to distill comedy and sometimes tragedy from the knockabout farce of people's outward behavior. Men and women as I see them would not be credible if they were literally transcribed; for instance . . . Captain Grimes in *Decline and Fall.* I knew such a man. . . . But had I written anything like a full account of his iniquities my publishers and I would have been in the police court. (8 April 1946)

Captain Grimes's progenitor, a man named Young, is introduced in Waugh's diary as someone who is "monotonously pederastic and talks only of sleeping boys" (14 May 1925). During the ensuing summer Waugh got to know Young better. In the diary he outlines Young's escapades as Young related them one evening which he and Waugh spent drinking together in a pub. Young, it seems, had been sent down from Oxford; he had left no fewer than four schools in mid-term as a result of a conviction of sodomy. "And yet he goes on getting better and better jobs without difficulty," Waugh concludes with bewilderment (3 July 1925). By the time Waugh dealt with Young in his autobiography, he had figured out why: "Headmasters were loath to admit that they had ever harbored such a villain, and passed him on silently and swiftly. He always emerged triumphant."[15] Grimes always does too, in *Decline and Fall*. "When you've been in the soup as often as I have," Grimes reflects in the novel, "it gives you a sort of feeling that everything's for the best, really."

Only one instance of Grimes's behavior in *Decline and Fall* is not based on Young's. When Grimes leaves his clothes, together with a suicide note, and swims out to sea (to give the impression he has drowned himself so that he can get clear once more), it is Waugh's own suicide attempt that the novelist describes.

Waugh's assertion, in his "Author's Note" to the original edition, that *Decline and Fall* is pure fiction is therefore hardly credible. His statement in the same note that the novel is not "a book with a purpose" but merely "meant to be funny" is likewise difficult to accept. Too many critics since have taken Waugh at his word, with the result that the novel has often been written off as a superficial satire. Elaine Bender, for example, finds "no norm or standard against which society is criticized. Such a standard is necessary for the best satire. The lack of an implicit theme makes the novel thin. It is all surface and jokes without any thematic substance. This is particularly distressing because the book demonstrates every other skill a comic novelist needs."[16]

On the contrary, *Decline and Fall* is a book very much endowed with a purpose, although it is admittedly a negative one. Through his hero, the hapless Paul Pennyfeather, Waugh shows innocence set adrift in a corrupt world where only the appearances of a Victorian morality remain. Though Waugh had shed his religious upbringing while at school, he was apparently beginning to believe on this eve of his conversion what he would often say explicitly thereafter: since modern civilization came into being through Christianity, it would not survive once its supernatural basis was removed.

In 1960 Waugh wrote an essay, never published, called "Man the Exile," which gives a succinct statement of his view of man in the modern world:

> Publicists flatter their readers and hearers by telling them that they live in an unique age. . . . This premise is false historically. The achievements of this age are negligible. To talk of the "conquest of space" is as inane as to say that man has "conquered" the sea when he has thrown a few pebbles in it. . . . The man of today is faced with the same problems (in different terms) as confronted his ancestors. . . . Individually each soul has his peace to make with his Creator. . . . Modern means of communication give a superficial emphasis . . . to what has basically been and always will be the natural (and supernatural) condition of man as an exile from Eden.[17]

These reflections echo Waugh's statement in 1939 that "man is, by nature, an exile and will never be self-sufficient or complete on this earth."[18] Man, as an exile from Eden, can only disintegrate in a society from which the values giving purpose to his existence have disappeared. The fact that Paul Pennyfeather does not disintegrate has a simple explanation: he is not a person but a device — the device Waugh uses to carry his reader along on a satirical sightseeing tour of a crumbling civilization. This alone can explain why Paul comes through his experiences totally unscathed and returns to divinity school (from which he was unjustly expelled for allegedly indecent behavior, at the beginning of the story). En route Paul has seen many signs of moral decay in modern society, exaggerated of course for purposes of satire.

In the first chapter, entitled "Vocation," Paul is expelled from college when some students steal his trousers. He sets out to be a teacher at Llanabba Castle in North Wales, run by the redoubtable Dr. Augustus Fagan, whose Ph.D. is as much a fake as the M.D. he later assumes. Fagan and the sodomite Grimes together provide an index of the state of affairs at Llanabba.

In expounding for Paul the guiding principles of his life, Grimes draws upon Robert Browning's poem "Mornings at Seven," which has often been called a distillation of the Victorian credo of optimism. "I don't pretend to be a particularly pious sort of chap," Grimes says, "but I've never had any Doubts. . . . You know, God's in His heaven; all's right with the world." The "Doubts" which Grimes refers to belong to Mr. Prendergast, another teacher at Llanabba, who left the ministry because of them:

> "You see, it wasn't the ordinary sort of Doubt about Cain's wife or the Old Testament miracles or the consecration of Archbishop Parker. I'd been taught how to explain all those while I was at college. No, it was something deeper than all that. *I couldn't understand why God had made the world at all.* . . . I asked my bishop; he didn't know. He said that he didn't think the point really arose as far as my practical duties as a parish priest were concerned."

Prendergast's advice from his bishop reminds one of how Waugh as a boy was told that his agnosticism would not interfere with his duties as sacristan at school. "Perhaps one day I shall see Light," Prendergast concludes, "and then I shall go back to the ministry."

Prendergast later becomes a "Modern Churchman" because as such he does not have to espouse any beliefs at all. He then takes a post as chaplain in the prison where Paul is later unjustly interned, since there is "more opening for a Modern Churchman in this kind of work than in the parishes." Waugh contrasts Prendergast's attenuated religious beliefs with the excessive religiosity of a fellow prisoner of Paul's who "looks daily for the Second Coming." The latter is disappointed that the chaplain, unlike himself, does not have visions: "Unworthy that I am, I am the Lord's appointed, . . . I am the sword of Israel; I am the lion of the Lord's elect."

In harmony with his efforts for prison reform, the inept warden of the prison gives to the "lion of the Lord's elect" some carpenter's tools so that the latter can pursue his craft. He pursues Prendergast instead, murdering him the next time the chaplain comes to visit. Thus one kind of distorted religious outlook has destroyed another.

Waugh's satire on Victorian mores is carried further in his representation of the *dolce vita* of England's decaying aristocracy, with whom Paul becomes embroiled. Lady Margot Beste-Chetwynde, to whom Paul becomes engaged, has maintained her fortune by operating the euphemistically titled Latin-American Entertainment Company, set up for traffic in white slavery. Paul's unwitting involvement in this operation brings his arrest on the eve of his wedding to Margot and his eventual imprisonment. Waugh's satire is at its most acrid when the judge, in passing sentence on Paul, berates him for attempting to tarnish a venerable aristocratic name by implicating "a lady of beauty, rank, and stainless reputation" in his nefarious activities.

An unmistakably religious air hovers about the social satire in *Decline and Fall*. But religion itself is not really being ridiculed at all — only religion in the bogus forms with which Paul comes in contact. Thus as the book ends, Paul has at last returned to divinity school to prepare for the priesthood and has retreated to a rigidly orthodox religious position — as far from Prendergast the Modern Churchman in one direction as from the "lion of the Lord's elect" in the other. In the last paragraph, Paul has settled down to study: "So the ascetic Ebionites used to turn towards Jerusalem when they prayed. Paul made a note of it. Quite right to suppress them." So ends the odyssey of Paul Pennyfeather.

The filming of Waugh's earliest novel by Twentieth Century Fox in 1968 inspired great anticipation in admirers of Waugh's fiction. To a large extent the product was not a disappointment. It was called *Decline and Fall of a Birdwatcher*, in an ill-advised attempt to distinguish it from an earlier movie based on Gibbon's *Decline and Fall of the Roman Empire*. Waugh approved the screenplay, Mrs. Waugh has told me, but of course did not approve the bogus title. Director John Krish caught the satirically solemn flavor of the original nicely, and the fine British cast rightly never cracked a smile in acting out Waugh's outlandish story. The film follows Waugh's lead in making its points in subtle satire rather than broad parody. Significantly, some of the funniest moments are those done just as Waugh devised them; the early portions, in which Paul is teaching in Dr. Fagan's school, for example, are among the best in the film just as they are in the novel.

Unfortunately producer-writer Ivan Foxwell decided to set the story in the present. This took the edge off much of the satire, since Waugh's thrusts were directed at the mindless gaiety of the Twenties. The result is rather like a modern-dress version of *Gone with the Wind* which makes no reference to the Civil War. Yet, though flawed by this one serious miscalculation, the film of *Decline and Fall* remains a faithful and generally entertaining rendition of Waugh's novel.

Vile Bodies (1930)

Throughout his fiction Waugh traces the course of his own generation. His heroes grow older as he does and, although Paul Pennyfeather never reappears in his fiction, several other characters from *Decline and Fall* do. For example Margot Beste-Chetwynde, now married to Lord Metroland, appears in Waugh's second novel, *Vile Bodies,* as well as in several other of his works, some at the end of his career. This continuity of characters gives Waugh's fiction an added dimension; one comes to feel immersed in the world of Evelyn Waugh. Still, as Waugh pointed out in the "Author's Note" to the original edition of *Vile Bodies,* the latter is "in no sense a sequel to *Decline and Fall,* though many of the same characters appear in both. I think, however, that some of the minor motives will be clearer to those who have read my first book than to those who have not."

Vile Bodies was published on 14 January 1930, while Waugh was thinking seriously of becoming a Catholic. The inscription in the copy which he presented to the Marston family that year reads, "From Evelyn Waugh. For this body which you call vile, my Lord Jesus Christ was not afraid to die!"[19] This inscription reflects how preoccupied Waugh was with religious matters at the time.

Waugh later devalued the novel as "a bad book, I think, not so carefully constructed as the first."[20] In the preface to *Vile Bodies* in the Second Uniform Edition Waugh calls the book "totally unplanned," explaining that "I had the faculty at the age of twenty-five to sit down at my table, set a few characters on the move, write three thousand words a day, and note with surprise what happened." Yet the novel was a success and caught the fancy of a public fascinated by Waugh's portrait of the last fling of the Bright Young People — the frivolous and frantic young set that characterized the Roaring Twenties in England. Waugh was chronicler of the demise of the Jazz Age in England just as F. Scott Fitzgerald was of its last glow in America.

"It was the first of my books to be a popular success," Waugh continues in his preface in the Second Uniform Edition. *Decline and Fall*, though well received, had sold fewer than three thousand copies in its first year. But the Bright Young People had since been popularized in the press; that guaranteed the success of *Vile Bodies*. Waugh considered himself on the fringe of this newsmaking group and remembers its members as "totally unlike the various publicized groups of modern youth, being mostly of good family and education and sharp intelligence; but they were equally anarchic and shortlived. The jargon most of us spoke came new to the novel reader," and some phrases such as "too sick-making" filtered into ordinary parlance. Because of the book's novelty, Waugh feels, its faults were overlooked; it reached the bestseller list because "there were not many comic writers at the time and I filled the gap."

Like *Decline and Fall*, *Vile Bodies* contains many satiric thrusts at the state of religion and morality in contemporary society. The first of these thrusts is delivered by Waugh in his "Author's Note," which points out that "Christmas is observed by the

Western Church on December 25th," as if the note were addressed to a tribe of aborigines. Man as an exile from Eden is epitomized in the central character — named, by no coincidence, Adam. Adam Fenwick-Symes's total lack of moral convictions is illustrated in his turning over his fiancée, Nina Blount, to a rival in exchange for having his hotel bill paid; he later retrieves Nina with a worthless check.

The mad existence he leads eventually becomes too much even for Adam. "Oh, Nina, *What a lot of parties,*" he exclaims at one point:

> "Masked parties, Savage parties, Victorian parties, Greek parties, Wild West parties, Russian parties, Circus parties where one had to dress as somebody else, almost naked parties in St. Johns Wood, parties in flats and studios and houses and ships and hotels and nightclubs, . . . parties at Oxford where one drank brown sherry and smoked Turkish cigarettes, dull dances in London and comic dances in Scotland and disgusting dances in Paris — all that succession and repetition of massed humanity. . . . Those vile bodies. . . ."

Waugh describes several such parties in his diary. On 29 December 1925, he mentions one of those "disgusting dances in Paris" which he attended at a "dreary looking café called Roland." After having had some drinks with a friend, Waugh was approached by a young man dressed as Cleopatra. He found the whole thing revolting. Waugh ends his account by noting that he took a taxi home "and went to bed in chastity. I think I do not regret it."

Waugh was clearly beginning to become disenchanted with the haphazard existence he was leading as one of the Bright Young People at this period. "Any sort of happiness or permanence seems so infinitely remote from any of us," he reflects in an entry dated February 1925. That word "permanence" plays an important thematic role in *Vile Bodies*.

The novel contains two religious figures: Father Rothschild, the wily Jesuit, and Mrs. Melrose Ape, the eccentric evangelist. Father Rothschild is a man of many paradoxes. For example, although he travels with a wealthy social set, he at times manifests some degree of asceticism; he is philosophic, for instance, about the rigors of sea travel: "To Father Rothschild no passage was worse than the other. He thought of the sufferings of the saints, the mutability of human nature, the Four Last Things, and between whiles repeated snatches of the penitential psalms."

It is Father Rothschild, moreover, whom Waugh employs to comment on the vagaries of the Bright Young People. At a party Prime Minister Outrage remarks to Father Rothschild that the younger generation had a chance after World War I which no generation has ever had: "There was a whole civilization to be saved and remade — and all they seem to do is to play the fool. Mind you, I'm all in favor of them having a fling. I dare say that Victorian ideas *were* a bit straitlaced." Father Rothschild replies:

> "I don't think people ever *want* to lose their faith either in religion or anything else. I know very few young people, but it seems to me that they are all possessed with an almost fatal hunger for permanence. I think all these divorces show that. People aren't content just to muddle along nowadays. . . . They say, 'If a thing's not worth doing well, it's not worth doing at all.' It makes everything very difficult for them."

Perhaps the *London Daily Express* had this passage in mind when it attempted to explain Waugh's conversion to Catholicism as an effort to escape the "queer cocktail world" of his novels by turning to a Church that offered satisfaction for the "universal longing for permanency" which people experience (30 September 1930). In any event, Waugh implies that Rothschild is not as "worldly" as he might appear.

Rothschild, says Father D'Arcy, "is a composite of several Jesuits — a satirical portrait. The legend still persists that Rothschild was based on myself, but I did not know Evelyn when he started the book." Waugh liked the Jesuits enough to poke a little good-natured fun at them; his portrait of Father Rothschild is his version of what he would later call "the 'wily Jesuit' of popular tradition."

The other representative of religion in *Vile Bodies* is Mrs. Melrose Ape (probably suggested by an American evangelist of the time, Aimée Semple McPherson), whose troupe of young female gospel singers are named Faith, Charity, Chastity, Humility, Prudence, Divine Discontent, Mercy, Justice, and Creative Endeavor. Their repertoire of hymns includes Mrs. Ape's own composition, "There Ain't No Flies on the Lamb of God."

Just as Captain Grimes had a less than wholesome interest in some of his students, so Mrs. Ape seems to have "favorites" among her girls. But regardless of her personal propensities and the histrionic way in which she conducts her services, there is enough truth in her performance to give at least the older members of the Lost Generation momentary pause. Mrs. Ape appears as the guest of honor at a party given by Margot Metroland, in a gown of heavy brocade "embroidered with texts." As the main event of the evening, she gives an oration on hope: "'Brothers and Sisters,' she said in a hoarse, stirring voice. . . . 'Just look at yourselves.' Magically, self-doubt began to spread in the audience. . . . Every heart had something to bemoan." Mrs. Ape's spell is quickly broken, however; so the party (and life) goes on as before.

Waugh makes his most searing comment on modern society as it is pictured in the novel when Nina goes for a ride in an airplane. Her companion intones an incorrect quote from Shakespeare as they survey the land below: "'This scepter'd isle, this earth of majesty, this something or other Eden. . . .'" After this casual reference to man's loss of Paradise, Waugh continues: "Nina looked down and saw inclined at an odd angle a horizon of straggling red suburb; . . . men and women were indiscernible except as tiny spots; they were marrying and shopping and making money and having children. The scene lurched and tilted again as the plane struck a current of air. 'I think I'm going to be sick,' Nina said." Nina's airsickness implies that the only genuine reaction to the topsy-turvy world which she sees below is revulsion.

Waugh based this scene on his own experience of flying in an early airplane, described in his first travel book, *Labels* (American title: *A Bachelor Abroad*). "I was sick into the little brown paper bag provided for me. One does not feel nearly as ill being air-sick as sea-sick; it is very much more sudden and decisive, but I was acutely embarrassed about my bag." As Waugh looked down on the city below, lying as it was "in a pool of stagnant smoke," he found that this "sombreness and squalor called up (particularly to me who had lately been sick) all the hatred and weariness which the modern megapolitan sometimes feels towards his own civilization."[22]

Such a world as Waugh pictures in *Vile Bodies*, a world whose external dirt and squalor betokens internal decay and corruption, must be purged. And so the final scene of the novel takes place in the midst of a war. Adam sits on a "splintered tree stump in the biggest battlefield in the history of the world." The scene all around him is "one of unrelieved desolation." There he encounters a girl who says that she was once called Chastity. She had gone off to South America to work for Margot Metroland's Latin-American Entertainment Company, but had returned when war broke out and has since been a camp follower. "Now I don't know where I am," she concludes. She is not the only one who is lost. A general whose car has broken down wanders by. "Damn difficult country to find one's way about in," he observes; "no landmarks."

Thus the novel ends with the characters wandering in an alien land, devoid of the landmarks that civilization once supplied. Adam, as lonely and desolate as the battlefield itself, tries to fall asleep, while Chastity is bedding down nearby with the general in the stranded car. The insistent sounds of the battle, which they try to ignore, are heard in the distance as the novel ends.

In a review of *Vile Bodies*, the *Saturday Review* criticized Waugh for dumping his characters into the middle of the next war the way Lewis Carroll's Alice was "dumped into the middle of next week," because he did not know what else to do with them (5 April 1930). On the contrary, Waugh seems to have established that the aimless and irresponsible pursuit of pleasure in which the Bright Young People have been engaged throughout the novel could only lead to disaster. This destiny was prefigured in Father Rothschild's remarks that there is "a radical instability in our whole world-order, and soon we shall all be walking into the jaws of destruction." The connection between the ensuing war and the dissolute lives of the Bright Young People is made more explicit in a later novel, *Put Out More Flags* (1942), when Alastair Trumpington joins the army as a kind of atonement for his mad youth.

Waugh's vision was darkened at this period by the anguish he felt in his divorce from his first wife, Evelyn Gardner. (I shall deal with his divorce later, in connection with *A Handful of Dust.*) Waugh notes cryptically in his preface to the Second Uniform Edition of *Vile Bodies*, "The composition of *Vile Bodies* was interrupted by a sharp disturbance in my private life and was finished in a very different mood from that in which it was begun. The reader may, perhaps, notice the transition from gaiety to bitterness." Indeed, one can hardly miss it.

The most ominous thing about the final scene of the novel is that Adam, Chastity, and the general are trying to ignore the approaching battle. We are left with the sad prospect that man may fail to profit by this cosmic purgation and survive only to repeat his past mistakes.

Black Mischief (1932)

The prospect foreshadowed in *Vile Bodies* is actualized in *Black Mischief*, which grew out of Waugh's first sojourn in Abyssinia as a newspaper correspondent. Waugh went to Abyssinia to cover the coronation of Emperor Haile Selassie for the *Daily Express* and went on to East and Central Africa before returning to England. His travel book *Remote People* (American title: *They Were Still Dancing*) and his novel *Black Mischief* both issued from his African adventures.

Black Mischief is set in Azania, which is a contraction of "Abyssinia" and "Zanzibar." Again Waugh treats the spiritual poverty of modern civilization. If western man himself cannot survive in a civilization deprived of its Christian underpinnings, certainly the veneer of western civilization which the Azanian emperior Seth (aided by the European missionaries) tries to impose on his people can only prove ludicrously incongruous. This incongruity is the basis of the novel's satire.

Seth's grandfather, Amurath, whom Seth eventually succeeds, was brought up a Nestorian but "declared Christianity the official religion of the Empire, reserving complete freedom of conscience to his Mohammedan and pagan subjects." Amurath encouraged an influx of missionaries, and soon three bishops were established in Azania: Anglican, Catholic, and Nestorian. "All this brought money into the new capital and enhanced his reputation abroad."

Once Seth comes to power, he continues his grandfather's halfhearted effort to maintain Christianity as the state religion. Seth characteristically fails to notice that the behavior of the Christian missionaries often is not very edifying. They hold themselves basically aloof from the crude common people and try to maintain the social amenities to which they have been accustomed back home.

Under the tutelage of Basil Seal, Waugh's roguish hero, Seth becomes interested in promoting birth control in Azania. Seth renames the site of the Anglican cathedral "Place Marie Stopes" — much to the subsequent dismay of the real-life Marie Stopes, a noted British advocate of birth control, who protested in the *Tablet* Waugh's use of her name (4 February 1933). Seth also decides to have a Pageant of Birth Control to encourage the practice. Waugh uses this as an occasion for satire aimed at the resident clergy. In the following passage, Waugh criticizes not only the gap which sometimes exists between public preaching and private practice but also the breakdown in that continuity of doctrine which was, for him, the hallmark of Catholicism:

> The Churches came out strong on the subject. No one could reasonably accuse the Nestorian Patriarch of fanatical moral inflexibility — indeed there had been incidents in his Beatitude's career when all but grave scandal had been caused to the faithful — but whatever his personal indulgence, his theology had always been unimpeachable. Whenever a firm lead was wanted on a question of opinion, the Patriarch had been willing to forsake his pleasures and pronounce freely and intransigently for the tradition he had inherited. . . . There was the painful case of the human sacrifices at the Bishop of Popo's consecration. . . .

On this and other uncertain topics the Patriarch had given proof of sturdy orthodoxy. But when Seth's birth control project ultimately fails, it is not because of church opposition but because too many of the ignorant poor entirely misunderstand the thrust of Seth's propaganda. They pour into the capital "eagerly awaiting initiation to the fine new magic of virility and fecundity."

To add to Seth's problems, it develops that Achon, the long-lost son of Amurath, has been found in the Monastery of St. Mark. Thus Achon (now close to ninety) and not Seth is the rightful ruler of Azania. The Nestorian Patriarch is confident that the monks will give Achon up for some "hard cash." This incident in the novel was triggered by an improbable story which, Waugh relates in *Remote People*, he heard reported as fact while he was in Abyssinia: that the real heir to the throne at the time of Haile Selassie's accession was hidden in the mountains, "fettered with chains of solid gold."[23]

Waugh's description of the Monastery of St. Mark is devastating in its satire of insincere religious practice, which inevitably degenerates into superstition and empty formalism:

The Monastery of St. Mark the Evangelist, though infected of late with the taint of heresy, was the center of Azanian spiritual life. Here in remote times Nestorian missionaries from Mesopotamia had set up a church and here when the great Amurath proclaimed Christianity the official creed of the Empire, the old foundations had been unearthed and a native community installed. . . . Here too were preserved among other relics of less certain authenticity, David's stone prised [pried] out of the forehead of Goliath, . . . and a wooden cross which had fallen from heaven quite unexpectedly during Good Friday luncheon some years back.

Waugh based his satirical description of the Monastery of St. Mark on the monastery at Debra Lebanos, which he visited while he was in Ethiopia. It was the center of Abyssinian spiritual life but, unlike its counterpart in *Black Mischief,* did not contain any notable relics, even of doubtful authenticity. Waugh's ever-dependable imagination, however, filled in the gaps when he was writing the passage just quoted.

After the right price is agreed upon by all parties, Achon is released. But the lengthy ceremonies of his coronation prove too much for the enfeebled Achon, who expires before they are over. Waugh's caustic comment on Haile Selassie's equally lengthy coronation ceremonies is succinctly put in his diary: "Interminable service, 6:30 – 12:30. Ritual made ludicrous" by the presence of newsreel cameramen (Coronation Sunday, 1930). In *Remote People* Waugh describes more fully how the clergy had shrewdly managed to expand the coronation ritual:

The six succeeding days of celebration were to be predominantly military, but the coronation day itself was in the hands of the church, and they were going to make the most of it. Psalms, canticles, and prayers succeeded each other, long passages of Scripture were read, all in the extinct ecclesiastical tongue, Ghiz.[24]

It is no wonder that Achon does not last through his interminable coronation ceremoney in *Black Mischief.*

In satirizing superstition and doctrinal confusion in *Black*

Mischief, Waugh was implicitly celebrating his own newfound faith, which he believed free of these limitations. But this implication escaped those of his readers who expressed dismay because they could discern no positive Christian values in the novel. Their dissatisfaction reached its peak in the controversy which surrounded the *Tablet's* attack on *Black Mischief*.

Years later Waugh was to refer to E. J. Oldmeadow, editor of the *Tablet* at the time of the controversy, as "a man of meagre attainments and deplorable manners, under whom the paper became petty in its interests and low in tone."[25] Oldmeadow refused to print a review of the novel and chose instead to castigate its author in an editorial:

> Whether or not Mr. Waugh still considers himself a Catholic, the *Tablet* does not know; but, in case he is so regarded by . . . novel-readers in general, we hereby state that his latest novel would be a disgrace to anybody professing the Catholic name. We refuse to print its title or to mention its publishers. (7 January 1933).

Two weeks later a group of Waugh's friends came to his defense in a joint letter to the *Tablet*, published January 21:

> Sir, — In a paragraph in your issue of January 7 you say of Mr. Evelyn Waugh that "his latest novel would be a disgrace to anybody professing the Catholic name." . . . We think these sentences exceeded the bounds of legitimate criticism and are in fact an imputation of bad faith. In writing, we wish only to express our great regret at their being published and our regard for Mr. Waugh.

M. C. D'Arcy, S.J.	Bede Jarrett, O.P.
T. F. Burns	D. B. Wyndham Lewis
Clonmore	C. C. Martindale, S.J.
Letitia Fairfield	R. H. J. Steuart, S.J.
Eric Gill	Algar Thorold
Christopher Hollis	Douglas Woodruff

Waugh at last entered the fray in May 1933, after Oldmeadow's references to *Black Mischief* had become progressively more insulting. The *Tablet* called the novel, among other things, nauseating, disgusting, and "a dunghill on which no lily could bloom." Waugh wrote an open letter to the Archbishop of Westminster, who at that time subsidized the *Tablet*. Waugh's letter was very specific in dealing with the charges brought against his novel. For example, near the end of the novel Basil Seal discovers that the main course served at a feast in which he has participated with the Azanian tribesmen has in fact been his girl friend Prudence. Since this passage was cited so often in the course of the controversy as being distasteful at best and immoral at worst, Waugh undertook to clarify his intent:

> Several writers whose opinion I respect . . . have told me that they regard this as a disagreeable incident. It was meant to be. . . . The story deals with the conflict of civilization, with all its attendant and deplorable ills, and barbarism. The plan of my book throughout was to keep the darker aspects of barbarism continually and unobtrusively present, a black and mischievous background against which the civilized characters performed their parts; . . . I introduced the cannibal theme in the first chapter and repeated it . . . thus hoping to prepare the reader for the sudden tragedy when barbarism at last emerges from the shadows and usurps the stage. It is not unlikely that I failed in this; that the transition was too rapid, the catastrophe too large.

As Frederick Stopp — to whom Waugh made the above letter available — has pointed out, the failing of the passage, if any, is artistic and not moral.[26]

Although Basil says at the end of the novel, "I think I've had enough of barbarism for a bit," Waugh had not finished with the topic. He dealt with it again in his next novel, *A Handful of Dust,* in his effort to drive home the point that civilization was growing closer to barbarism as it drifted farther away from Christian values.

Waugh's first three satirical novels were fundamentally lighthearted books growing out of relatively happy experiences. Though Waugh had gone through the anguish of his divorce during the composition of *Vile Bodies,* it was only when he turned to *A*

Handful of Dust that he sought to deal with this intimate experience in fictional terms. As he did so his satire took on the more serious tone that was to mark his last prewar work of fiction, *Work Suspended*, and his first war novel, *Put Out More Flags*, and would ultimately characterize the serious fiction of his later career.

Before considering *A Handful of Dust* and the novels that followed, therefore, I shall consider the experience of Waugh's first marriage and divorce, which contributed notably to the gradual darkening of his personal vision — a process that was to continue to the end of his life.

3

Change and Decay: Further Satires

Evelyn Waugh met Evelyn Gardner, to whom he was to be married for less than a year, at a party in the spring of 1927; they were engaged that December.

To Alec Waugh, Evelyn Gardner seemed a charming woman, "pretty and neat and gracious":

> She and Evelyn were a delightful team; they were so at ease, so affectionate together, their having the same Christian name was an amusing bond. They were called "He-Evelyn" and "She-Evelyn." But of course from every worldly point of view, it was a ridiculous engagement.

Her mother, Lady Burghclere, was not impressed by Waugh's lack of prospects for a respectable career. She made inquiries at Oxford about her prospective son-in-law. C. R. M. F. Cruttwell, dean of Waugh's college, with whom Waugh had constantly feuded during his Oxford days, took great satisfaction in performing the "unwelcome duty" of telling Lady Burghclere that Mr. Waugh was not a fit suitor for her daughter.[27] Evelyn later took his revenge on Cruttwell by giving that name to several disreputable minor characters in his fiction; but that was no solace at the time.

Arthur Waugh, Evelyn's father, had a frank conference with Lady Burghclere, who finally gave her reluctant consent to the marriage; but there was to be no announcement of the betrothal in the *Times*. Meanwhile Evelyn had thought to better his situation by arranging through his old college friend Anthony Powell to publish a life of Rossetti for Duckworth's, where Powell was employed. In 1926 Evelyn had published a brief study called *P.R.B.: An Essay on the Pre-Raphaelite Brotherhood*, which he was now able to expand into a biography of Rossetti for the sum of fifty pounds. "I was delighted," Evelyn said later, "as fifty pounds was quite a lot then. I dashed off and dashed it off. The result was hurried and bad." Yet the book, published in 1928, was well noticed in the *Times Literary Supplement* in a review that was complimentary to the book's author, "Miss Waugh."

There was an implicit understanding that if Evelyn's first novel, *Decline and Fall*, was as well received as his biography of Rossetti, opposition to his marrying Evelyn Gardner would cease. *Decline and Fall*, published the same year, was indeed critically successful and Waugh's wedding took place secretly. "Evelyn and I were married at St. Paul's, Portman Square, at twelve o'clock," Waugh notes in his diary for 27 June 1928. "A woman was typewriting on the altar." Alec Waugh acted as a witness.

Waugh stoically recounts the aftermath: "I went through a form of marriage and travelled about Europe for some months with this consort. I wrote accounts of these travels which were bundled together into books and paid for the journeys, but left nothing over."[28] In a situation later approximated by a fictional one in *A Handful of Dust*, Mrs. Waugh stayed on in their London flat while her husband went to the country to work on his second novel, *Vile Bodies* (1930). While he was away she fell in love with John Heygate, a young man at the BBC whom Alec found "a perfectly pleasant fellow. . . . He was not particularly good-looking. He was not particularly anything." (The first Mrs.

Waugh's second marriage was to prove as short-lived as her first.)

Alec discussed the impending divorce with his brother, who commented at the close of their discussion, "The trouble about the world today is that there's not enough religion in it. There's nothing to stop young people doing whatever they feel like doing at the moment." This thought was to permeate *A Handful of Dust*. Alec later reflected, "I have no doubt that the break-up of his marriage hastened his conversion to the Roman Catholic faith."[29]

A Handful of Dust (1934)

After his divorce Waugh took to traveling, since he had "no fixed home and no possessions which could not conveniently go on a porter's barrow."[30] The later chapters of *A Handful of Dust* originated in one of these expeditions, as he recounts in the preface to the novel in the Second Uniform Edition:

> This book found favor with the critics who often date my decline from it. It had confused origins. In January, 1933, I was travelling alone in the borderlands of British Guiana and Brazil. . . . I came to an impasse at the Brazilian village of Boa Vista and spent the tedious days of waiting for a non-existent boat in writing a short story which was later published under the title "The Man Who Liked Dickens." That story was substantially the chapter of this book named "Du Côté de Chez Todd." A year passed. I was wintering at Fez in Morocco and there I wrote this novel, on the theme of the betrayed romantic, affording an explanation of my hero's presence in the South American bush.

"Eventually," Waugh wrote in his *Life* essay "Fan-Fare" (8 April 1946), the story grew into "a study of other sorts of savage at home and the civilized man's helpless plight among them." At one point Tony Last, the novel's hero, converses with his brother-in-law, Reggie St. Cloud, on the subject of civilization. Of his research Reggie says, "Why, ten years ago I couldn't be interested in anything later than the Sumerian age and I assure you that now I find even the Christian era full of significance" (that is, as a historical curiosity).

The absence of a meaningful religion in touch with contemporary man's needs is underscored in the character of Reverend Tendril, the local vicar, whose services Tony occasionally attends in order to edify the locals, since he is lord of the manor. The vicar, having served in India most of his life, still gives unaltered the sermons he once delivered to the troops in the garrison chapel. For example, in his usual Christmas sermon the vicar speaks of a Christmas spent under the "harsh glare of the alien sun. . . . Instead of the ox and ass of Bethlehem . . . we have for companions the ravening tiger and the exotic camel." The villagers do not find the vicar's sermons inappropriate, since "few of the things said in church seemed to have any particular reference to themselves."

Just how irrelevant religion has become in Tony's life is demonstrated when his small son John is killed in a riding accident. Tony finds dealing with the vicar about the funeral distasteful rather than consoling: "I only wanted to see him about arrangements," says Tony. "He tried to be comforting. It was very painful. . . . After all the last thing one wants to talk about at a time like this is religion."

Tony's estranged wife Brenda lives in a flat in London in order to be near her lover, John Beaver. Eventually Tony and Brenda decide to get a divorce. It is only in the midst of the divorce proceedings that Tony becomes aware of the disorder and chaos which surround him:

> For a month now he had lived in a world suddenly bereft of order; it was as though the whole reasonable and decent constitution of things, the sum of all he had experienced or learned to expect, were an inconspicuous, inconsiderable object mislaid on the dressing table; no outrageous circumstance in which he found himself, no new mad thing brought to his notice could add a jot to the all-encompassing chaos that shrieked about his ears.

Tony's yearning for order is reflected in his accepting Mrs. Rattery's invitation to play cards, for "under her fingers order grew out of chaos; she established sequence and precedence; the symbols before her became coherent, interrelated."

In the 1930s it was thought good form for the husband to allow his wife to divorce him, even though she might be the guilty party. Waugh refused to follow this cavalier convention in his own case and sued his wife for divorce. In *A Handful of Dust* he burlesques the notion that the husband should take the rap for his wife's infidelity by creating a hilarious episode in which Tony Last tries to do "the gentlemanly thing" by being "discovered" with a woman in a seaside resort.

Tony engages a rather disreputable lawyer who specializes in divorce cases. He sends Tony to a seedy hotel where "the servants are well accustomed to giving evidence." To complicate the proceedings further, the girl with whom Tony is to spend the weekend insists on bringing along her small daughter. The little girl has to be coaxed to stay out of the way so that Tony can get on with the formalities of providing evidence for the divorce case.

Brenda's lawyer rounds off the charges against Tony by including in her divorce petition a statement that her "erring spouse" is a dissolute drunkard as well as a lecher, to impress the judge all the more. "A great deal depends on psychological impression," the lawyer insists. "Judges in their more lucid moments sometimes wonder why perfectly respectable, happily married men go off for weekends to the seaside with women they do not know. It is always helpful to offer evidence of general degeneracy." The bitterness of Waugh's own divorce is hardly veiled in this remark.

After Tony's divorce from Brenda, the mysterious Dr. Messinger convinces Tony to go with him to South America in search of a Lost City; he then deserts Tony in the jungle. As the South American journey proceeds, we become aware that Tony's Lost City is not the City of God. Tony's "quest" is in fact a retreat from his unhappy experiences into a more gentle past. He finally realizes that this is impossible. As he lies delirious in the hut of Mr. Todd, the half breed who has found him unconscious in the jungle, he mumbles, "There is no City." John Beaver's mother, an interior decorator of garish taste, "has covered it with chromium plating and converted it into flats . . . very suitable for base love." This is the world in which Brenda thrives and in which Tony, the betrayed romantic, cannot survive. Tony is now in the hands of Mr. Todd (whose name very likely comes from Tod, German for "death"). As the novel closes, Tony can only look forward to living out his days reading and rereading Dickens to Mr. Todd, with no hope of returning home.

The idea of "a man trapped in the jungle, ending his days reading Dickens aloud" to a madman came to Waugh quite easily, he recalls in his Life essay "Fan-fare" (8 April 1946), "from the experience of visiting a lonely settler of that kind and reflecting how easily he could hold me prisoner." This meeting took place while Waugh was traveling in the Brazilian jungle and preparing to write another travel book, Ninety-Two Days. The man's name was Christie. "Arrived at Christie's ranch at 4:00. He was warned of a stranger in a dream," Waugh's diary reads for 20 January 1933.

In chapter three of Ninety-Two Days Waugh elaborates the bizarre conversations in which he engaged with Christie and which he neatly summarizes in his diary, as in the following excerpt: "Questioned him about theology. 'Believe in the Trinity? I couldn't live without them. But they are no mystery. It is all quite simple.'" Waugh ends his account of his sojourn with this religious fanatic by describing how he dozed off during one of Christie's endless disquisitions on theology to his large family circle. The first time Waugh awoke his host was clarifying visions and mystic numbers for his listeners. "When I next awoke they had all gone away, but I could hear Mr. Christie prowling round in the darkness outside and muttering to himself."[31] Christie was indeed a suitable model for Mr. Todd in A Handful of Dust.

In addition to the ending described earlier, *A Handful of Dust* has an alternative ending that replaces chapters five through seven of the standard text. In his preface to the 1964 Second Uniform Edition of the book, Waugh explains how *A Handful of Dust* came to have two endings: "An American magazine wished to serialize the novel (under a title of their choosing, *A Flat in London)* but could not do so while it incorporated 'The Man Who Liked Dickens.' I accordingly provided the alternative ending," which is appended to the 1964 British edition in addition to the original ending as "a curiosity." In the alternative ending, Brenda returns to Tony after John Beaver has left her for another woman. Tony returns safely from his trip but secretly takes over the flat which Brenda had kept in London for her trysts with John Beaver for his own private use in the future.

Both endings show Tony betrayed by his romantic illusions and hence disillusioned with life. Whether we last see Tony intending to get even with Brenda by betraying her or languishing in Mr. Todd's hut after he has failed to find his Lost City, he remains lost in the alien land and hostile jungle of which Reverend Tendril spoke in his Christmas sermon. In both endings to the novel Waugh makes the point that the ideals Tony has tried to live by are no match for the forces in the modern world with which he must cope. Ultimately, Tony is betrayed not just by Brenda, Messinger, and Todd but by his empty Victorian code of morality, which has lost its grounding in religious belief. Tony is therefore not so much the betrayed romantic as the betrayed humanist. In fact, in his *Life* essay Waugh called this novel "humanist" and said that it "contained all I had to say about humanism."

Scoop (1938)

In contrast to *A Handful of Dust* with its sober implications about modern life, Waugh next wrote what he calls (in his pref -ace to the 1964 edition of the novel) a "light-hearted tale," generated by the "peculiar personal happiness" which he was enjoying at the time that he wrote it. (Waugh is referring, of course, to his marriage to Laura Herbert, which I shall treat later in this chapter.) The earliest editions of *Scoop* bore the subtitle *A Novel about Jurnalists,* but Waugh subsequently deleted this phrase from the title because he found it superfluous. It had been added originally, he explains in his 1964 preface, because at the time the novel was first published foreign correspondents enjoyed "an unprecedented and undeserved fame," and his publisher thought that the subtitle would increase the book's sales.

I rather wish that Waugh had retained the subtitle, since it emphasizes that the target of the book's satire is not so much the African nation where the story takes place as the newspaper profession itself. In this sense Waugh could have changed the setting to another country altogether and still included most of the satire he aims at the reporters in the book. Waugh chose to deal in the novel with journalists in a foreign capital; he himself had recently done a stint in Abyssinia as a foreign correspondent for the *Daily Mail* at the outbreak of the Italo-Ethiopian War in 1935, and had written about his experiences in *Waugh in Abyssinia* (1936). "I had no talent for this work," he confesses in his preface to *Scoop*, "but I joyfully studied the eccentricities and excesses of my colleagues," which he made the basis for the humor of the novel — one of the funniest books he ever wrote.

The geographical location of Waugh's fictional state of Ishmaelia is exactly the same as that of Abyssinia, he says, "and the description of life among the journalists in Jacksonburg is very close to Addis Ababa in 1935." Regarding his eccentric hero William Boot and Boot's equally eccentric family at Boot Magna, Waugh points out that "younger readers must accept my assurance that such people and their servants did exist quite lately and are not pure fantasy."

If Waugh considered himself something less than competent as a foreign correspondent, he has created a hero whose ineptitude for the job is monumental. Drawing on his growing preference for country life, Waugh pictures William Boot in safe seclusion at the crusty old family estate of Boot Magna. Here Boot writes a regular column for the *Daily Beast* called "Lush Places," in which he seeks to enable the harried London commuter to share vicariously the joys of country life.

William's solitude, too good to last, is shattered when he is summoned to London for an interview with the paper's publisher, Lord Copper. William has just discovered that his sister, in typing his essay about the badger, had mischievously substituted for the name of that nasty little animal the name of the great crested grebe, a rare and beautiful bird which clearly does not deserve the contempt that William intended to bestow on the badger. William is certain that Lord Copper has gotten wind of this calamity and is going to fire him.

The truth is that John Courtney Boot, an aspiring writer caught in one of the recurring crises of his love life, has asked his good friend Julia Stitch to use her influence with Lord Copper to get him sent to cover the Ishmaelian situation. John wants to get out of England until his amorous affair has blown over. Julia, as wealthy as she is scatterbrained, agrees to help him, but by mistake she manages to have William — not John Courtney — appointed to represent the *Beast* in Ishmaelia.

In a later travel book, *Tourist in Africa,* Waugh describes a friend "whom I have more than once attempted to portray in fiction as 'Mrs. Stitch,'" and whom he identifies in his diary as his old friend Lady Diana Cooper. The way Waugh describes Lady Diana in *Tourist in Africa* indicates that Mrs. Stitch's real-life counterpart was somewhat eccentric too. Waugh tells of meeting her in Genoa in 1959 at a time when she was busy running errands for some friends she had left behind in Rome. Lady Diana was engaged in reclaiming from the Lost and Found Department of a railway depot "a coat of unlovely squalor, abandoned somewhere by one of her irresponsible cronies, without authority or means of identification." Yet she was able to cajole "a series of beaming officials and possessed herself of the sordid garment."[32]

In *Scoop* Mrs. Stitch is involved in a hilarious scene in which she loses control of her car and drives it into a public rest room for men. This is the type of person who, without knowing it, has taken a hand in controlling the destiny of William Boot. For his part William, like the hero of Samuel Taylor Coleridge's "Rime of the Ancient Mariner," senses the bird which he has offended is somehow having him punished for the ugly article he published about it. Hence William accepts his fate and consents to go off to Ishmaelia to meet his destiny, just as Waugh set out for Abyssinia in 1935.

Since the crisis in Abyssinia prompted worldwide concern, journals everywhere had dispatched representatives to Addis Ababa. In lines he might well have included in *Scoop*, Waugh recalls in *Waugh in Abyssinia* the feverish efforts of journalists to cash in on the sudden international interest in Abyssinia's imminent war with Italy: "Travel books whose first editions had long since been remaindered were being reissued in startling wrappers. . . . Files were being searched for photographs of any inhospitable-looking people — Patagonian Indians, Borneo headhunters, Australian aborigines — which could be reproduced to illustrate Abyssinia." In this mad atmosphere, says Waugh, even he could obtain employment in the "unfamiliar but not uncongenial disguise" of a war correspondent, although he had "an inkling of what later became abundantly clear to all, that I did not know the first thing about being a war correspondent."[33]

Some of the journalists he met once he arrived on the scene, however, evidently had no more experience than he did. One Spaniard confided to him that he had brought along a good history of Africa written in German: "When I have nothing to report, I translate passages from that." It is no wonder that Waugh the novelist began making mental notes for the novel that he intended to base on his observations of his journalistic colleagues once he had written his nonfiction account of his stay.

Waugh was able to transfer some incidents that he had recorded in *Waugh in Abyssinia* directly into *Scoop* with little variation. In *Waugh in Abyssinia,* for example, he described the method by which telegrams were distributed as a procedure which gave limitless opportunities for loss and delay: they were delivered by messengers who could not read and whose system of delivery therefore was to hand a bundle of envelopes to the first white man they saw. The latter would read all the telegrams that looked promising and finally hand back to the messenger the ones that were not for him. Here is·how Waugh the novelist makes use of this same material in *Scoop:*

> Telegrams in Jacksonburg were delivered irregularly and rather capriciously, for none of the messengers could read. The usual method was to wait until half a dozen had accumulated and then send a messenger to hawk them about the more probable places until they were claimed.

Without Waugh's description of the same procedure in *Waugh in Abyssinia,* the reader of *Scoop* might well assume that this absurd method of mail delivery in Jacksonburg was too farfetched to be anything but the product of Waugh's satirical imagination. Fact, it seems, can be just as comical as fiction.

By the same token, Waugh's acrid remarks in *Waugh in Abyssinia* about dishonest reporting match anything that occurs in *Scoop.* There was only one slight difference, he discovered, in the professional codes of English and American journalists: "While the latter will not hesitate in moments of emergency to resort to pure invention, the former must obtain their lies at second hand. This is not so much due to lack of imagination, I think, as lack of courage." As long as someone, no matter how irresponsible or previously discredited, had provided some information, Waugh found, it was considered legitimate news and enabled the British journalist to preface his dubious report with "It is stated in some quarters" or "I was unofficially informed." It was on that "unofficial source," accordingly, that any subsequent blame was fixed.[34]

Into this corrupt world of foreign correspondents Waugh

introduces his hapless hero, William Boot, in *Scoop*. William has an intimation of the kind of situation in which he is to be enmeshed when Lord Copper gives him his last orders that William's reports are to be based on the premise that the Patriots are right and are going to win and that the *Beast* is standing behind them four-square: "A few sharp victories, some conspicuous acts of personal bravery on the Patriot side, and a colorful entry into the capital. That is the *Beast* policy for the war."

But when William later attempts to find out which of the factions battling in Ishmaelia is considered to be the Patriot side, he is informed by Mr. Salter, one of Lord Copper's subordinates, that both sides call themselves Patriots and that both sides will claim all the victories. "But of course," Salter adds, "it's really a war between Russia and Germany and Italy and Japan who are all against one another on the patriotic side. I hope I make myself plain?" Fortified with this background material, William embarks on his career as a journalist.

One of his fellow reporters in Ishmaelia, a man named Corker, takes William under his wing, telling him not to worry if his reports contradict those filed by other correspondents, since all of the papers have different policies and therefore expect different news. This consideration offers William some consolation. He nonetheless endeavors to keep his diminishing grip on reality intact, despite the fact that the Ishmaelian government further complicates his efforts to file genuinely accurate news reports by issuing false public statements to prevent the correspondents from finding out what really is going on.

In one scene William steadfastly refuses to join the other journalists in a trip to a place which the government has designated a potential trouble spot, because he has learned from other sources that no such place exists. When he confronts a government official with this discrepancy, the official only shrugs, "I see you are well informed about my country, Mr. Boot. I should not have thought it from the tone of your newspaper." To make matters worse, William is besieged by cables from the *Beast* which remind him that "Lord Copper personally requires victories" and order him to cable victories "until further notice."

William never does figure out which faction the *Beast* considers to be the Patriots, to whom he is to attribute all of the victories. However, the British vice-consul does inform him that His Majesty's Government is rooting for the Jackson family, the party in power, who are willing to negotiate with Britain rather than Russia about Ishmaelia's mineral deposits. The Jacksons, he is told, suit the country and suit His Majesty's Government. William's own patriotism is now aroused and he goes back to his hotel to cable the *Beast* to back the Jacksons for the good of England.

In the funniest single paragraph in the entire book Waugh describes William laboriously typing out his message, possessed with sentiments of patriotism and zeal for justice: "One finger was not enough; he used both hands. The keys rose together like bristles on a porcupine, jammed, and were extricated; curious anagrams appeared on the paper before him; vulgar fractions and marks of punctuation mingled with the letters. Still he typed." Back at the *Beast's* office the editor reads William's cable and is lost in admiration for Lord Copper's shrewd choice of William as the paper's correspondent in Ishmaelia.

In the wake of William's report Mr. Baldwin, a British emissary to the Ishmaelian government, parachutes into the capital and closes the deal for the mineral deposits. Mr. Baldwin is based on Mr. F. W. Rickett, whom Waugh met in Abyssinia. Unfortunately for Waugh the correspondent, Waugh was not in Addis Ababa when Rickett, representing a group of American financiers, secured from Emperor Haile Selassie a concession of valuable mineral rights which Italy would otherwise have tried to annex. Somewhat wistfully, Waugh the novelist allows William Boot to have the scoop which he himself missed.

William returns home in triumph, but the comedy of errors is not over yet. When he refuses to attend a banquet that Lord Copper has arranged in honor of "Boot of the *Beast*," William's

Uncle Theodore is asked to join the staff of the newspaper; and the celebration goes on as scheduled with Uncle Theodore as guest of honor. In addition, as a result of Mrs. Stitch's charmingly muddled intervention, a knighthood, likewise originally intended for William, is conferred on John Courtney Boot by mistake.

William does not mind, however, because he is left to retire once more to Boot Magna and compose "Lush Places." We last see him engaged in this very activity, picturing how "maternal rodents pilot their furry brood through the stubble." Significantly Waugh adds, "Outside the owls hunted maternal rodents and their furry brood." The world beyond William's study, he suggests, is not the lush place William likes to imagine it. Waugh knew that in 1938 war clouds were gathering in places much closer than far-off Ishmaelia. Hence, although William's seclusion at Boot Magna can be termed pure escapism, Waugh obviously did not endorse his behavior.

The realities of life cannot be wished away, Waugh implies, although he very likely agreed with the sentiments expressed in the hymn Uncle Theodore was fond of humming: "Change and decay in all around I see." The critic Alain Blayac comments that as Waugh's fiction began to show the influence of his religious conversion, he in effect moved on to the next line of the hymn: "O Thou, who changes not, abide with me."[35]

Waugh's becoming a Catholic involved a great sacrifice of which many people were unaware. His friend Reverend Martin D'Arcy pointed out to me: "When his wife left him for another man less than a year after they were married, it was a terrible blow to his pride and very hard to forgive. After Evelyn had gotten a divorce, he knew that if he became a Roman Catholic he would have to give up all hope of remarrying and having children, something which he wanted very much." Nevertheless, he did join the Church with this understanding. Not until six years later was the possibility of an annulment of his first marriage broached to him. In the intervening years, 1930 to 1936,

Waugh spent most of his time traveling. In addition to providing material for travel books, Waugh's peregrinations gave him background on which he drew for his novels, especially *Black Mischief, A Handful of Dust,* and *Scoop.*

One evening in 1936, after Waugh had settled down once more in England, he was discussing his unfortunate first marriage over a glass of wine with some close friends. Someone suggested he might have grounds for an annulment since, as Douglas Woodruff would later comment in his obituary of Waugh in the *Tablet,* Waugh's was the kind of marriage which could not be described as having been intended by *both* parties as an indissoluble Christian union (16 April 1966). Father D'Arcy recalls:

Evelyn came to me about it and I took his case to the ecclesiastical authorities, who quickly said that there was no marriage. I then prepared Evelyn's petition to Rome to have his marriage annulled. Months passed and no word. Finally a friend of mine in the cardinal's office in London checked and found that Evelyn's petition was in a desk drawer and had never been sent to Rome. I was worried that Evelyn would become very disillusioned with the Church. He wrote to me that he realized that I was getting anxious about him, but that I should set aside my fears; he said that no matter how "discreditable" the ecclesiastical authorities turned out to be, his faith was completely intact. When Cardinal Hinsley took over the diocese, a new man was put in charge of the marriage court and he took care of Evelyn's case very rapidly. Within a few months Evelyn had his answer from Rome. His marriage was annulled.

In April 1937 Waugh married Laura Herbert, a Roman Catholic who was a cousin of his first wife. Lady Victoria Herbert, the same grandaunt who had objected to Waugh's marrying Evelyn Gardner, now exclaimed, "What, this young man again, I thought we'd seen the last of him."[36] "Laura was a lovely girl," says Father D'Arcy, "wonderful in handling all of his moods."

Waugh's diary for 17 April 1937 says simply, "Early Mass. Changed and pick-me-up and to church where got married to Laura." The following day, the first of their honeymoon, the diary continues in the same tone of contentment: "Lovely day, lovely house, lovely wife, great happiness." Waugh and his new wife bought a house in Gloucestershire called Piers Court and became accustomed to a quieter kind of life than Waugh had led during the restless years of travel after his divorce. But still he was aware that the insistent rumblings of war would intrude at least temporarily on the quiet life he had now constructed.

Work Suspended (1942)

Work Suspended is the aptly titled unfinished novel which Waugh worked on before the beginning of World War II. More than any other of Waugh's novels, it was a dress rehearsal for *Brideshead Revisited*. "So far as it went, it was my best writing," he wrote in his dedication to Alexander Woollcott at the time of *Work Suspended*'s publication. Waugh nevertheless abandoned the project because "the world in which and for which it was designed, has ceased to exist." With the coming of World War II and his eventual entrance into the service, Waugh lost interest in working on a novel about the prewar period and published it as a fragment. Nevertheless, the uncompleted novel left its mark on Waugh the writer. Here, for the first time in Waugh's fiction, the hero serves as narrator of his own story, a device which Waugh was to perfect in *Brideshead Revisited*.

The hero of *Work Suspended* is John Plant, a writer of detective fiction trying unsuccessfully to finish his latest novel. John is no luckier in love, for he loses his girl to Roger Simmonds. Her conversion to Marxism coincides with her falling in love with Roger: "She and Roger had been to meetings together, and together read epitomes of Marxist philosophy. Her faith, like a Christian's, was essential to her marriage." Thus, ever so casually, Waugh introduces the theme of how disagreements over religious faith can prove a potential obstacle to marriage, a theme which was to be so prominent in *Brideshead Revisited*.

Work Suspended ends where Waugh's next novel, *Put Out More*

Flags, begins: with the coming of World War II changing the lives of all of the characters. "And so an epoch, my epoch, came to an end," says John; it presages a new life not of their own contriving for John and his friends. "Our story, like my novel, remained un- finished — a heap of neglected foolscap at the back of a drawer." But though John's novel remains unfinished, *Work Suspended* it- self was to be completed, in a sense, under a different title and with other characters. In Charles Ryder, hero of *Brideshead Revisited,* there is much of John Plant, the sensitive artist who loses his love to another man and goes off to war alone. John Plant asks himself the question that must be answered before Waugh can have Ryder narrate *Brideshead:* "To write of someone loved, of someone loving, above all of oneself being loved — how can these things be done with propriety?"

Put Out More Flags (1942)

Meanwhile Waugh turned his attention to *Put Out More Flags,* which the critic William Cook rightly calls a transitional novel; it employs characters from Waugh's earlier novels, such as Basil Seal, yet looks forward to the more serious situations and more genuinely human characters of the fiction to come.[37] "This is the only book I have written purely for pleasure," Waugh said of it afterwards in his preface to the 1966 Second Uniform Edition of the novel. In the summer of 1941, "after the fall of Crete, the Commandos in the Middle East were disbanded, and officers and men returned to their regiments. I found myself in a comfort- able liner, full below decks with Italian prisoners, returning to the United Kingdom and to my wife and children." Since he had only negligible duties, he wrote all day, "and the book was finished in a month." The characters about whom he had written in the previous decade came to life for him once more: "I was anxious to know how they had been doing since I last heard of them, and I followed them with no preconceived plan, not knowing where I should find them from one page to the next."

Waugh ends his preface by remarking that "I did, in the first weeks of the war, before I got my commission, suffer severely from 'evacuees.'" "I remember our family's staying at my grandmother's home later in the war," says Waugh's oldest daughter, Teresa, "and my father would come down and visit us on brief leaves and observe how the local people were billeting the evacuees from the big cities that were being bombed. This became the source of one of the episodes in *Put Out More Flags*."

Here is how it all began: "Evacuated children here today," Waugh wrote in his diary on 2 September 1939, two days before the outbreak of the war in Europe. He describes them as "hanging round the village looking very bored and lost." Waugh found the children more and more of a nuisance as time went on, as two later diary entries suggest: The evacuees who remain "spend their leisure scattering waste paper round my gates" (8 September 1939); "Work out of the question as the evacuated children are now admitted to the garden at the back of the house under my windows. Impetigo, thrush, and various ailments are rampant" (19 October 1939).

Waugh distilled his irritation at the evacuees into one of the most comical incidents in *Put Out More Flags*, centered about the Connolly children: Doris, a tomboy; Mickey, an incipient delinquent; and Marlene, a mental defective. Since none of the otherwise generous inhabitants of the village will have them, the redoubtable Basil Seal, a billeting officer, concocts a plot whereby he transports them round the countryside demanding a bribe from each resident before he will transfer the trio to the nearest neighbor.

"The longest that the Connollies stayed in any place was ten days; the shortest was an hour and a half." One of their temporary hosts tells Basil that he had actually considered giving the Connollies a dose of weed-killer. "That would be one way," Basil says thoughtfully. "Do you think that Marlene could keep it down?" Having realized a tidy sum by the time he has made the rounds of his territory, Basil finally turns the Connollies over to

44

Mr. Todhunter, the billeting officer in a nearby zone — for a price, of course — and Todhunter carries on this lucrative venture in his own territory.

In his dedication of the novel to Randolph Churchill, Waugh referred to Basil Seal and the others whom he reemployed in this novel as a "race of ghosts, the survivors of the world we both knew ten years ago. . . . Like everyone else they have been disturbed in their habits by the rough intrusion of current history." In time of crisis people often rejuvenate discarded convictions and beliefs, almost in spite of themselves, as something to hold on to. This reaction marks several of Waugh's characters, most notably Ambrose Silk and Alastair Trumpington, as it did many of his friends at that time.

The war causes Ambrose Silk, the homosexual esthete, to take stock of his convictions. He muses on the workers' paradise envisioned by his Communist companions and on the Christian heaven he had learned about as a child, either of which would be "absolutely uninhabitable for anyone of civilized taste." Since he cannot make up his mind about a religious commitment, Ambrose quite fittingly becomes the sole representative of atheism in the Religious Department of the Ministry of Information. Here he shares a room and a secretary with "a fanatical young Roman Catholic layman, . . . a bland non-conformist minister, and a Church of England clergyman." Ambrose's task is to supply copy for periodicals like *Free Thought*, *Atheist Advertiser*, and *Godless Sunday at Home*.

It is difficult not to like Waugh's benighted Ambrose and his ilk. One could easily apply to these characters what Waugh himself wrote of Graham Greene's characters in *Commonweal*:

> The children of Adam are not a race of noble savages who need only a divine spark to perfect them. They are aboriginally corrupt. Their tiny relative advantages of intelligence and taste and good looks and good manners are quite insignificant. The compassion and condescension of the Word becoming flesh are glorified in the depths. (16 July 1948)

As Waugh presents these children of Adam, we not only like them but even on occasion feel compassion for them. For example, Waugh treats sympathetically Ambrose Silk's tragic friendship with the storm trooper Hans, a relationship which prefigures that of Sebastian and Kurt in *Brideshead Revisited.* Ambrose recalls:

> Hans loving his comrades, finding in a deep tribal emotion an escape from the guilt of personal love, Hans singing with his Hitler youth comrades, cutting trees with them, making roads, still loving his old friend, puzzled that he could not fit the old love into the scheme of the new.

When Hans's storm trooper comrades inevitably discover that Ambrose is a Jew, Ambrose must flee back to England alone.

Passages of this sort show that Waugh's approach to his material was gradually becoming more serious; perhaps he was trying to prepare himself for a novel that would be serious throughout. In *Put Out More Flags*, Ambrose eventually becomes comic again as Basil uses a false pretext to pack him off to Ireland disguised as an Irish Jesuit, so that he can take over Ambrose's apartment. But one cannot forget the serious tinge Ambrose's character took on, if only briefly, a few pages earlier in the novel.

Ambrose Silk was obviously based on Brian Howard, a notoriously degenerate homosexual acquaintance from Waugh's Oxford days. Howard had already served as the source of the social-climbing Johnny Hoop in *Vile Bodies* and would later appear in the guise of Anthony Blanche in *Brideshead Revisited.* Howard not only recognized himself in Ambrose Silk but also was able to identify Hans as his own German friend Toni and was deeply offended by Waugh's treatment. Although Howard's irritation with Waugh is understandable, the character Waugh depicted in *Put Out More Flags* was, by all accounts, much more likable and sympathetic than his counterpart in real life.

As Robert Murray Davis writes in a sketch of Howard's life, while in the foreign service during World War II Howard made it clear that he hated "officers, clerics, and 'failed gentlemen,' and he seems to have pursued his contacts through a great many bars, making loud threats to denounce as fascists anyone who incurred his displeasure."[38] Still, in fairness to Howard, perhaps Waugh should not have drawn on his personal life and propensities quite as obviously as he did. After receiving similar complaints from acquaintances who resented his portrayal of them, the American novelist Thomas Wolfe reflected that one could depict a character as a horsethief, "but you do not need to give his real address and telephone number."[39]

Even the characters not based on real people seemed to take on a life of their own, Waugh found as he was writing *Put Out More Flags*. "As for my characters, I have very little control of them," he wrote in his *Life* essay "Fan-fare." "I start them off with certain preconceived notions of what they will do and say in certain circumstances, but I constantly find them moving another way." One of the characters in *Put Out More Flags*, Angela Lyne, who had married for wealth and position but secretly loves Basil Seal, illustrates this point: "I had no idea until halfway through the book that she drank secretly. I could not understand why she behaved so oddly. Then when she sat down suddenly on the steps of a cinema I understood all and I had to go back and introduce some empty bottles into her flat." It was while discussing the novel at lunch one day with a fellow officer aboard the troop ship that Waugh suddenly got this insight and blurted out, "I know. Mrs. Lyne has been drinking!"

Waugh was beginning to add depth to his characterizations by the time he wrote *Put Out More Flags*. Alastair Trumpington is perhaps the most roundly drawn character in the novel. Alastair is profoundly influenced by the coming of the war, for he looks upon the war as an opportunity to serve his country. He has come a long way, obviously, from the drunken student he was when he helped steal Paul Pennyfeather's trousers in *Decline and Fall*. However hazy his motivation, Alastair realizes from the start that he and his irresponsible generation did nothing to avert the coming catastrophe. When he hears that war has been declared, he immediately feels ashamed to be found lounging away a Sunday in his pajamas with a jug of ale: "It was as though he had been taken in adultery at Christmas or found in mid-June on the steps of Bratt's in a soft hat."

While Basil Seal aspires to nothing more than being "one of those people one heard about in 1919: the hard-faced men who did well out of the war," Alastair joins the regular army instead of putting in for a commission as his knighthood might dictate. To Sonia, his wife, he confides, "We've had a pretty easy life up to now. It's probably quite good for one to have a change sometimes." This gives Sonia the key to his action as she later explains it to Basil:

> You see he'd never done anything for the country and though we were always broke we had lots of money really and lots of fun. I believe he thought that perhaps if we hadn't had so much fun perhaps there wouldn't have been any war. Though how he could blame himself for Hitler I never quite saw. . . . At least I do now in a way. . . . He went into the ranks as a kind of penance or whatever it's called, that religious people are always supposed to do.

Not wishing to overrate Alastair's sacrifice, however, Waugh adds, "It was a penance whose austerities, such as they were, admitted of relaxation." Besides, Alastair eventually joins his peers as an officer. Nonetheless, a refugee from the Bright Young People is here taking something of an unselfish attitude toward his country's crisis. The fervor of this patriotic fever even infects Basil, who announces in anticipation, "There's only one serious occupation for a chap now, that's killing Germans. I have an idea I shall rather enjoy it."

David Lodge, the contemporary British novelist, complains in his monograph on Waugh that he finds the change of heart exhibited by Basil and the other aging Bright Young People in this national emergency to be implausible, for a heart is "an organ which, in the past, they showed few signs of possessing."⁴⁰ Perhaps men like Alastair, no longer able to live without faith in something, tacked the remnant of their religious faith onto the war banner and made patriotism their one solid virtue: For King and Country if not for God and Country. As for Basil, his motivation is always questionable, whatever he undertakes. Things may have gotten too hot for him at the War Office, where he has pulled off more than one nefarious operation for his own advancement. Besides, Basil has a chance of joining the same company as Alastair and Peter Best-Chetwynde (Paul Pennyfeather's former pupil and Margot Metroland's son, now Earl of Pastmaster).

According to a novella Waugh published in 1962 called *Basil Seal Rides Again*, Alastair dies honorably in battle, thus vindicating his original noble aspirations. According to the same story, Basil's military career is cut short by injuries sustained while (quite characteristically) he was demonstrating an untrustworthy explosive devise of his own invention.⁴¹ However, Basil's mother, Lady Seal, has no doubt that the Bright Young People of yesterday will be the heroes of tomorrow as they go off to fight the Germans: "I am not quite sure what they are going to do," she opines to her friend Sir Joseph Mainwaring, "but I know that it is very dashing and may have a decisive effect on the war." "There's a new spirit abroad," agrees Joseph, "I see it on every side." "And, poor booby," Waugh adds in the last line of the book, "he was bang right."

That new spirit spreads to other characters in the novel as well. One of them, a poet named Parsnip who is probably a caricature of W. H. Auden, is working on an opus called *Guernica Revisited*. He is having difficulties with it, and his friends decide that his writing must take account of the ongoing war. One friend, Julia Stitch, remarks, "When we say Parsnip can't write in wartime Europe, surely we mean that he can't write as he has written up till now." Thus, in the midst of his wartime novel *Put Out More Flags*, Waugh hints that the sobering experiences which war entails will prompt him to write a novel very much different from the full-length novels he had written up to this point, a new kind of novel to which *Work Suspended* had already pointed the way.

This novel, *Brideshead Revisited*, the most serious and soul-searching of his works thus far, became to Waugh's complete surprise the greatest popular success of his career. "Now, unseasonably," Waugh wrote with some bewilderment in his *Life* essay of 8 April 1946, "like a shy waterfowl who has hatched out a dragon's egg, I find that I have written a 'best-seller.'"

To many critics *Brideshead Revisited* seemed a departure from the lighter type of fiction they had come to expect from Waugh. Yet a shrewd observer of his fiction could hardly miss the serious elements in *A Handful of Dust*, *Work Suspended*, and *Put Out More Flags* that signaled Waugh's intent of creating a serious novel of some depth. In that novel, *Brideshead Revisited*, Waugh was to attempt for the first time to encapsulate his own religious convictions, for mature consideration by a world recently emerged from war.

4

The Purpose Revealed: Waugh's Central Novel

When *Brideshead Revisited*, Waugh's first explicitly religious novel, appeared in 1945, many readers assumed that he had experienced his religious conversion shortly before writing it. Actually only two of Waugh's novels, *Decline and Fall* and *Vile Bodies*, were completed before he entered the Roman Catholic Church. Why had his religious frame of reference not been evident in his earlier work? Immediately after his conversion in 1930, as his daughter Teresa D'Arms pointed out to me, "My father became a newspaper correspondent and travelled all over the world; then came the war and he went into the army. Up to that point his immediate experience had provided the material for his fiction."

Waugh's war experiences had a sobering effect on his outlook, prompting the kind of reflection that went into his more serious fiction. "With the war," says his son Auberon Waugh, "he became older and more serious." It was understandable, therefore, that Waugh's religious vision, which had been developing steadily since his conversion, would at last find expression in his fiction.

Alec Waugh does not carry his recollections of his brother in *My Brother Evelyn* past the point at which Evelyn considers the possibility of joining the Catholic Church. "I cannot enter imaginatively into the mind of a person for whom religion is a crusade," he explains elsewhere. "You cannot appraise a stained-glass window if you look at it from the outside."[42] Alec has written to me in a similar vein: "My brother and I never discussed his conversion, and in my piece about him in *My Brother Evelyn* I was careful to break off my narrative at the point of his conversion. I have no doubt that his Catholicism colored and gave depth and purpose to all his writing."

Evelyn Waugh's religion had a profound influence on his writing, especially on *Brideshead* and later novels. What brought about his conversion, and what role did it play in his life and work? When I asked his friend Father D'Arcy what factors he felt contributed to Waugh's conversion, he replied that some of Waugh's set at Oxford had been Catholic; for example, Harold Acton, who had an Italian Catholic background, impressed Waugh very much. In addition, "Evelyn was attracted at the time to Olivia Plunkett-Greene, the daughter of Gwendoline Plunkett-Greene, who was in turn the niece of the prominent German Catholic theologian, Baron Von Hugel. Gwendoline, who later became a Catholic herself, wrote *Mount Zion*, a book of spiritual reflections which impressed Evelyn more than he realized at the time."

It was Waugh's Oxford friends who introduced him to the Jesuits at Farm Street Church in London (which figures in *Brideshead Revisited*) and later to Father D'Arcy, master of Campion Hall, the Jesuit College at Oxford. Waugh began taking instructions in the faith from Father D'Arcy in July 1930. "Went to Father D'Arcy at 11," Waugh's diary reports on 8 July 1930. "Blue chin and fine slippery mind." Waugh found the Jesuit residence at Farm Street where they met to be "superbly ill-furnished. Anglicans can never achieve this ruthless absence of 'good taste.'"

"Evelyn didn't join the Catholic church for its ritual," Father

D'Arcy explains; "he had already found the liturgical services and architectural feats of the Anglican church to his liking." In Waugh's own words:

> The medieval cathedrals and churches, the rich ceremonies that surround the monarchy, the historic titles of Canterbury and York, . . . the liturgy composed in the heyday of English prose style — all these are the property of the Church of England, while Catholics meet in modern buildings, often of deplorable design, and are usually served by simple Irish missionaries.

What did impress Waugh about Roman Catholicism was its historical continuity:

> England was Catholic for nine hundred years, then Protestant for three hundred, then agnostic for a century. The Catholic structure still lies lightly buried beneath every phase of English life; history, topography, law, archaeology everywhere reveal Catholic origins. . . . It only remained to examine the historical and philosophic grounds for supposing the Christian revelation to be genuine. I was fortunate enough to be introduced to a brilliant and holy priest who undertook to prove this to me, and so on firm intellectual conviction but with little emotion I was admitted into the Church.[43]

"Yes, it was an unemotional conversion," Father D'Arcy agrees. "Evelyn basically believed that God had revealed himself through Christianity. He wanted to understand the nature of the Good News of salvation. He wanted Catholicism explained with complete clarity and objectivity. His conversion was not the product of emotional upheaval. He wanted to understand the faith and he maintained this attitude all his life."

The sincerity of Waugh's decision to join the Catholic church is mirrored in an undated letter he wrote to Father D'Arcy shortly before embarking on a trip to Ireland, while he was still taking instructions:

> I wonder whether it will be possible for me to continue my instructions when I get back from Ireland. Shall you be in Oxford? I could

easily come to live there or near there for a time. As I said when we first met, I realize that the Roman Catholic Church is the only genuine form of Christianity. Also that Christianity is the essential and formative constituent of western culture. In our conversations and in what I have read or heard since, I have been able to understand a great deal of the dogma and discipline which seemed odd to me before. But the trouble is that I don't feel Christian in the absolute sense. The question seems to be must I wait until I do feel this — which I suppose is a gift from God which no amount of instruction can give one, or can I become a Catholic when I am in such an incomplete state — and so get the benefit of the sacraments and receive faith afterwards?

Father D'Arcy managed to dispel Waugh's misgivings and the latter was received into the Catholic church at the age of twenty-six on 29 September, 1930.

In an editorial in the *Daily Express,* Waugh's conversion was compared to that of other British writers such as G. K. Chesterton:

Another British author has been received into the Roman Catholic Church. . . . Is it that the post-war novelists seek refuge from their own writings, that deal so exclusively with their queer little cocktail world? Or is it that the swiftly changing conditions of today create a universal longing for permanency, for a Church that refuses to do honor to compromise? (30 September 1930)

Shortly after his conversion, Waugh wrote an essay for the same newspaper setting forth publicly some reasons for his conversion:

Civilization . . . has not the power in itself of survival. It came into being through Christianity, and without it has no significance or power to command allegiance. . . . It is no longer possible, as it was in the time of Gibbon, to accept the benefits of civilization and at the same time deny the supernatural basis upon which it rests. . . . Christianity exists in its most complete and vital form in the Roman Catholic Church. I do not mean any impertinence to the many devout Anglicans and Protestants who are leading lives of great devotion and benevolence; I do find, however, that other religious bodies, however fine the example of certain individual members, show unmistakable signs that they are not fitted for the conflict in which Christianity is engaged. . . . For instance, it seems to me a necessary sign of completeness and vitality in a religious body that its teaching shall be coherent and consistent. If its own mind is not made up it can hardly hope to withstand disorder from outside.[44]

"Disorder from outside" was later to be most concretely embodied in the Nazi threat which precipitated World War II. An incident that occurred while Waugh was taking a course at a company commanders' school in Scotland illustrates that Waugh's religious convictions did not waver. Waugh was undergoing a routine psychological examination at the school which, he says in his diary, was conducted by "a neurotic creature classed as a major who tried to impute unhappiness and frustration to me at all stages of adolescence. He neglected to mention religion and I gave him a little lecture about that at the end" (January 1942). According to Eric Linklater, who knew Waugh at this time, Waugh asked the psychiatrist why he had omitted any questions about religion, which he considered to be "the most important of all the agents that form a man's character."[45]

Feeling as he did about religion's role in man's psychic life, Waugh naturally made room for religion in the next novel he wrote, one in which he tried to analyze the psychology of his characters more thoroughly than he ever had before.

Brideshead Revisited (1945)

How Waugh found time to write such an ambitious work as *Brideshead Revisited* in the midst of army service warrants some explanation, and he provides it in the preface to *Brideshead Revisited* in the Second Uniform Edition of 1960:

In December, 1943, I had the good fortune when parachuting to incur a minor injury which afforded me a rest from military service. This was extended by a sympathetic commanding officer, who let me remain unemployed until June, 1944, when the book was finished. I wrote with a zest that was quite strange to me and also with impatience to get back to the war.

The commanding officer in question was Colonel William Stirling, who said years later that he had realized that Waugh, idle with a bad leg and wanting to write a book, might prove a "disruptive influence" on the military unit: "It was difficult if one was doing a general reorganization of things to have to deal with Evelyn as well. . . . So I saw my chance, and perhaps slightly outside the official regulations, I said to Evelyn, . . . 'Come back when you've finished your book or when I send for you.'"[46]

From January to June 1944 Waugh composed *Brideshead* at a hotel at Chagford, Devon. On May 9, for example, he recorded in his diary that he had finished an arduous fourteen-thousand-word chapter: "In spite of some passages of beauty I am not sure of my success." By June 6, however, the author was more confident about his progress. At breakfast he learned of the Allies' D-day invasion, which had begun that morning, but he was undistracted by the news and sat down to write "a fine passage of Lord Marchmain's death agonies. . . . I sent for the priest to give Lord Marchmain the last sacraments" and wound up the chapter by 4 P.M. "I took it to the post and walked home by the upper road. There only remains the epilogue which is easy meat."

By the time the page proofs of the novel were ready, Waugh had returned to active service and had been dispatched to Yugoslavia; the proofs were parachuted to him there for correction. "I corrected proofs in the cold of my bedroom," his diary notes (21 November 1944). As Waugh himself recounts it, the set of proofs "was sent in October, 1944, . . . to 10 Downing Street, from there it travelled to Italy in the Prime Minister's post bag, was flown from Brindisi and dropped by parachute, . . . was corrected at Topusko and taken . . . by ship to Italy, and so home, via Downing Street."[47]

The subtitle, "A Household of the Faith," borne by an early draft of the novel, indicates the spiritual dimensions the novel had assumed for Waugh. The household referred to is that of the

Marchmain family. When *Brideshead* was published after the war, Waugh prefaced the first British edition with a "Warning," just as he had done in the case of the first British edition of *Decline and Fall* in 1928. But whereas Waugh had "warned" readers of *Decline and Fall* that the book was meant to be funny, he felt obliged to "warn" readers of *Brideshead Revisited* that this book was not meant to be funny:

> There are passages of buffoonery, but the general theme is at once romantic and eschatological. It is ambitious, perhaps intolerably presumptuous; nothing less than an attempt to trace the workings of Divine purpose in a pagan world, in the lives of an English Catholic family, half-paganized themselves, in the world of 1923-39. The story will be uncongenial alike to those who look back on that pagan world with unalloyed affection, and to those who see it as transitory, insignificant, and, already, hopefully passed. Whom, then, can I hope to please? Perhaps those who . . . look to the future with black foreboding and need more solid comfort than rosy memories. For the latter I have given my hero, and them, if they will allow me, a hope, not indeed that anything but disaster lies ahead, but that the human spirit, redeemed, can survive all disasters.

Brideshead proved a best-seller when it appeared in 1945, and in America probably had more readers than all of his previous books put together. Nevertheless some of the critics who had admired Waugh's early satires were baffled and disappointed by the serious religious overtones of *Brideshead*. This novel, says Waugh in his 1960 preface, "lost me such esteem as I once enjoyed among my contemporaries and led me into an unfamiliar world of fan-mail and press photographers."

Edmund Wilson was the most vituperative of those critics who thought *Brideshead* too radical a departure from Waugh's previous work. In response Waugh wrote in *Life* magazine:

> Mr. Edmund Wilson, who once professed a generous interest in me . . . was outraged (quite legitimately by his standards) at finding God introduced into my story. I believe that you can only leave God out by making your characters pure abstractions. . . . The

failure of modern novelists since and including James Joyce is one
of presumption and exorbitance. . . . They try to represent the
whole human mind and soul and yet omit its determining
character — that of being God's creature with a defined purpose.

Waugh then stated flatly that in his future novels, just as in
Brideshead, he would continue to try to represent man more fully,
"which, to me, means only one thing, man in his relation to God"
(Life, 8 April 1946).

Yet, despite the success of the novel, Waugh was not entirely
satisfied with the book. As early as 1950 he mentioned in a letter,
"It might interest you to know that my summer task is a complete
rewriting of *Brideshead Revisited.*"[48] His publishers, however, over-
ruled him at the time, and not until 1960 did Waugh publish the
revised British edition. In the new preface Waugh states that the
novel's theme, "the operation of·divine grace on a group of di-
verse but closely connected characters," still seems to him to be
presumptuously large; but he makes no apology for it.

One of Waugh's principal aims in revising the novel was to
strengthen the unity of the book so that this theme, missed by
many readers, would emerge more clearly. He divided the first of
the original two sections of the novel into two parts. Book I keeps
its original title, "Et in Arcadia Ego" ("I Am Even in Arcadia"), and
treats of the hero Charles Ryder's student days at Oxford. The
new Book II is called "Brideshead Deserted" and deals with
Ryder's time at Brideshead. What was originally Book II now becomes Book III and retains its original title, "A Twitch Upon the
Thread." It takes us through Ryder's marriage years. Waugh also reinstated the original chapter headings of the 1945 British
edition, this time placing them at the beginning of each chapter as
well as in the table of contents. Waugh had originally added the
chapter headings to the page proofs in his own hand, directing
that they appear only in the table of contents. But there they
were easily overlooked. (They have never appeared in any American edition of the novel.) The most significant of these chapter
titles is the one attached to the last chapter before the epilogue —
"The Purpose Revealed."

Among what Waugh calls in the preface the "substantial cuts" he made to tighten the unity of the novel is the deletion of the purple patch of writing at the beginning of Book III, in which the Marchmain family is compared to an aboriginal race that has gone through a period of crisis and then sunk into obscurity. Waugh also made "small additions," some of which help prepare the reader for the sections about religious experiences that climax the novel. (I shall treat some of these emendations in detail as I discuss the novel.)

Brideshead begins with a prologue in which Captain Charles Ryder revisits the Marchmain family mansion of Brideshead after it has been taken over during World War II for use by the army. He recalls the Marchmain family and the many years in which their lives mingled with his. We see each of them, then, as Charles remembers them and in relation to the role they have played in his life. Thus Charles's memories of his days at Oxford with Sebastian, younger son of the family, appear more idyllic than they really were since Charles is recalling them amid the privations of World War II. Yet even in his Oxford days Charles kept in his room a skull with the inscription "Et in Arcadia Ego" on its forehead, as a reminder that in this imperfect world our days in the Arcadia of youth are numbered. Charles is willing to accept this fact but Sebastian, his closest friend at Oxford, is not. Sebastian later travels as far as Morocco trying to recapture something of the carefree life which he had known at Oxford with Charles. The character of Sebastian bears Waugh's own nostalgic recollections of Oxford and is a combination of at least two of Waugh's contemporaries there: Hugh Lygon, Waugh's roommate at Oxford, and Keith Douglas, who (like Sebastian) carried a huge teddy bear with him wherever he went.

Waugh scatters little hints here and there in the early part of the book regarding the religious theme which he is developing in his story. For instance, Charles's cousin Jasper, who preceded him at Oxford, warns Charles, "Beware of Anglo-Catholics — they're all sodomites with unpleasant accents. In fact, steer clear of all the religious groups: they do nothing but harm." But

Charles does make friends with Sebastian and enters into a relationship with Sebastian's Catholic family that is to bring him spiritual growth through suffering and sacrifice.

The comic muse who served Waugh so well in his previous novels does not desert him in *Brideshead Revisited*, despite the book's overall seriousness, for some of its humorous characters are reminiscent of his earlier work. One such character is Anthony Blanche, Sebastian's eccentric homosexual friend; Anthony, like Ambrose Silk in *Put Out More Flags*, was based on the notorious Brian Howard. The critic John Hardy finds these individuals mere "refugees" from Waugh's earlier work who do not belong in the more serious world of *Brideshead*.[49] But, on the contrary, satirical creations such as Anthony and Charles's pompous father provide comic relief that is welcome in the serious milieu of *Brideshead*. Furthermore, these characters are purposely drawn by Waugh in the superficial manner customary for a comic character; thus they provide a background against which the more completely realized principal characters of the novel stand out. This is also true of the humorous characters in Waugh's later serious novels, including the *Sword of Honor* trilogy.

The comic sequences in which characters like Anthony are involved — such as the incident at Oxford in which his fellow students dunk him in a fountain but discover to their chagrin that he has immensely enjoyed being manhandled — reflect the fact that even a novel with a strong religious theme must be anchored firmly in the human comedy. Otherwise the work fails to imply that the realm of the spirit is involved with the world of everyday reality and that the two interact. As Father D'Arcy puts the problem, in a work of art which has a religious theme divine grace must be shown working amid "the hurly-burly of human life."

Significantly, when Anthony describes Sebastian's family to Charles he paints them as if they were characters from Waugh's early satires. How else indeed could Anthony see them than as refugees from his own proper milieu? According to Anthony, Sebastian's father, Lord Alex Marchmain, is a Byronic figure. He is estranged from his wife, Lady Theresa Marchmain, and lives on the continent with his middle-aged mistress, Cara. Lady Marchmain is the "Reinhardt nun" who has "convinced the world that Lord Marchmain is a monster. . . . She refuses to divorce him because she is so pious," and because, of course, her Catholic religion does not approve of divorce. Sebastian's sister, Julia, a debutante, is too charming for Anthony's taste: "There ought to be an Inquisition especially set up to burn her." Sebastian's brother Brideshead, a conservative man in life and outlook, is "something archaic," a "learned bigot." Finally, about the youngest member of the family, Cordelia, who is still in school, Anthony can only say, "I'm sure she's abominable."

Even allowing for Anthony's customary hyperbole, Charles suspects that there might be something in what he says; but he goes to Brideshead as Sebastian's guest anyway. When the reader, along with Charles, actually meets the Marchmains as the novel progresses, he finds them taking on the dimensions of fully drawn human beings, dimensions which the minor comic characters in the novel lack. Nevertheless, the minor characters (such as Charles's father) further the action of the plot as well as provide diversion. For example, Charles and his father regard each other with veiled hostility rooted in the generation gap that separates them. This hostility manifests itself in the witty verbal battles they wage whenever Charles is home. Later in the novel Waugh uses Charles's estrangement from his father to help explain why Charles becomes so close to Sebastian and Julia's father, Lord Alex, and is therefore so affected by the latter's deathbed conversion.

Waugh was careful not to overdo the comic function of Charles's father, however, for he deleted from the page proofs of *Brideshead* an entire episode in which the elder Ryder figures. The episode begins with Charles's bored attendance at a dinner party which his father has arranged before Charles can leave to visit Brideshead. As part of the evening's entertainment one guest, Miss Pomfrey, does a series of dreary imitations. To get even with his father for the wretched evening, Charles invites Miss Pomfrey to return for Sunday luncheon to perform again for his father, who has a sacrosanct custom of dining alone on Sundays which probably survives, says Charles, "from the sabbatarian practices of our forebears." His father contrives to be absent for the luncheon but advises Charles that Charles should give Miss Pomfrey a remuneration for her performance, since she was not really a guest at the party but a paid entertainer. In the course of their luncheon together Charles learns that she is no such thing and that had he offered her money it would have been very embarrassing indeed. On his return home that afternoon, the elder Mr. Ryder admits that through his "hoax" he had intended to get even with Charles for spoiling his Sunday luncheon.

This episode loses a great deal in paraphrase, since Waugh narrates it in a very understated and witty fashion which brings out the uneasy relationship between father and son. Charles's relationship with his father mirrors that which Waugh experienced with his own father, which he recalled in an essay for the *Sunday Telegraph*, "My Father." "We were never intimate in the sense of my coming to him with confidences or seeking advice," he remembers. "Our relationship was rather that of host and guest" (2 December 1962). Indeed, no better phrase could be used to describe Charles Ryder's superficial rapport with his father in *Brideshead* than "host and guest."

At this time in the story Charles is an agnostic (he corrects Sebastian when the latter playfully calls him an atheist) and finds Sebastian's obvious religious faith an enigma, "but not one which I felt particularly concerned to solve. I had no religion. I was taken to church weekly as a child, and at school attended chapel daily." Here Waugh makes a crucial change in the original text. In the revised edition he inserts the following lines:

> My father did not go to church except on family occasions and then with derision. My mother, I think, was devout. It once seemed odd to me that she should have thought it her duty to leave my father and me and go off with an ambulance, to Serbia, to die of exhaustion in the snows of Bosnia. But later I recognized some

such spirit in myself. Later, too, I have come to accept claims which then, in 1923, I never troubled to examine, and to accept the supernatural as the real. I was aware of no such needs that summer at Brideshead.

The question, What motivated Charles in his ultimate acceptance of religious faith? is as much literary as theological, for Waugh would have failed as a novelist had he not provided sufficient motivation for Charles's decision. Charles's conversion is foreshadowed in the story by the profound religious regeneration which three of the Marchmains undergo in the course of the novel. The experiences of Sebastian, Lord Alex, and Julia Marchmain (each to be examined in turn) thoroughly prepare the reader for Charles's change of heart.

First there is Sebastian. Charles finds it curious that although Sebastian seldom performs any religious acts such as going to mass, he makes a chance remark almost every day that reminds Charles he is a Catholic. Charles tries to look upon this as a foible — like the teddy bear Aloysius which Sebastian makes his constant companion — until one day Sebastian says absentmindedly, "Oh dear, it's very difficult being a Catholic. . . . Who was it used to pray, 'Oh God, make me good, but not yet'?" Sebastian then tries to describe for Charles's benefit the part religion plays in the life of each member of his family. For example, his brother Bridey had once wanted to be a Jesuit: "There was a frightful to-do — monks and monsignori running around the house like mice, and Brideshead just sitting glum and talking about the will of God. He was the most upset, you see, when papa went abroad." Sebastian concludes:

"So you see we're a mixed family religiously. Brideshead and Cordelia are both fervent Catholics; he's miserable, she's bird happy; Julia and I are half-heathen; I am happy, I rather think Julia isn't; mummy is popularly believed to be a saint and papa is excommunicated — and I wouldn't know which of them was happy. Anyway, however you look at it, happiness doesn't seem to have much to do with it, and that is all I want."

When Sebastian says that happiness is all he wants, he does not realize how difficult it is going to be for him to achieve. Cara, Alex's mistress, is of course aware that his immaturity will be his chief obstacle to fulfillment. She remarks to Charles, "Sebastian is in love with his own childhood. That will make him very unhappy. His teddy bear, his Nanny . . . and he is nineteen years old."

Sebastian has already begun to drink heavily. Gradually he sinks into both dipsomania and homosexuality. In order to escape his mother's excessive influence, he flees to Morocco where he forms an attachment to a shiftless German, Kurt. Charles tracks Sebastian down but decides he can do nothing to help since Sebastian intends to stay in Morocco with Kurt. "You know, Charles," Sebastian explains, "it's rather a pleasant change when all your life you've had people looking after you, to have someone to look after yourself. Only of course it has to be someone pretty hopeless to need looking after by *me*."

Cordelia goes to visit Sebastian after working with the ambulance corps in the Spanish Civil War. She finds that he has returned to the Church; indeed, he has become very religious since the fathers of a monastery near Carthage found him starving on their doorstep and took him in. In a variation on the story of Ambrose and Hans in *Put Out More Flags*, Kurt has been forced into the German army as a storm trooper but deserted to be with Sebastian and finally hanged himself after being captured and sent to prison.

Cordelia says that the monks will let Sebastian stay on in the monastery, though not as a member of the order: "There are usually a few odd hangers-on in a religious house, you know; people who can't quite fit in either to the world or the monastic rule. I suppose I'm something of the sort myself. But as I don't happen to drink, I'm more employable." To Charles's surprise she tells him that the monks consider Sebastian a very holy man as the result of his sufferings. But Cordelia is not surprised: "No one is ever holy without suffering. . . . It's the spring of love."

Cordelia obviously has her mother's piety. Lady Theresa Marchmain is a devout Catholic; she is also a possessive woman, and her overprotective attitude toward Sebastian is one of the things that drove him away. Furthermore Alex, her estranged husband, hates her, though his mistress Cara does not think that Lady Marchmain is all to blame. Alex fell in love with Lady Marchmain before he had reached maturity; for him it was a kind of puppy love which turned to hatred when he eventually outgrew it. "She has done nothing except be loved by someone who was not grown up," says Cara. In hating his wife, "Alex is hating all the illusions of boyhood — innocence, God, hope."

Cordelia almost seems to be taking up Cara's train of thought when she tells Charles:

"I sometimes think when people wanted to hate God they hated mummy. . . . Well, you see, she was saintly but she wasn't a saint. No one could really hate a saint, could they? They can't really hate God either. When they want to hate Him and His saints they have to find something like themselves and pretend it's God and hate that."

After Lady Marchmain has died, Alex returns to Brideshead to live out his last days. This prompts the crisis that leads to the climax of the story. Charles is appalled that the Marchmain family wants Alex to see a priest on his deathbed, since Alex has quite plainly repudiated his faith. Charles says angrily, "They'll come now, when his mind's wandering and he hasn't the strength to resist, and claim him as a death-bed penitent." The priest, Father Mackay, feels that by the grace of God Alex may repent. Father Mackay, an unimpressive man, exemplifies Waugh's belief that, as he once expressed it in the *National Review,* a priest's personal foibles "serve only to emphasize the mystery" of his unique calling (4 December 1962). While Father Mackay is with Alex, Charles becomes aware that the priest has ceased to be the "simple, genial man" Charles had known before and has taken on a quiet solemnity of which Charles never thought him capable. Alex is apparently in a coma when Father Mackay gives him absolution for his sins and anoints him with the oil of the Sacrament of the Sick. Alex's hand moves slowly to his forehead; for a moment he seems about to wipe away the oil, but he is really making the sign of the cross. That evening he dies.

Alex's return to the Catholic church on his deathbed has been severely criticized by many as unconvincing. In Waugh's defense, Reverend Martin D'Arcy notes that Waugh once told him of assisting at just such a deathbed repentance. "Hence," says Father D'Arcy, "the final repentance of Alex in *Brideshead Revisited* had its genesis in a real-life incident."

In fall 1943 Waugh's good friend Hubert Duggan, brother of the novelist Alfred Duggan, was taken fatally ill. Waugh, who happened to be in London on leave, went to see him before he died. As in the case of Alex Marchmain in *Brideshead*, some members of Duggan's family resisted the suggestion that he see a priest before the end. Waugh, however, was adamantly in favor of it. "I went to Farm Street and brought back Father Devasse," he writes in his diary. "Father Devasse, very quiet and simple and humble, trying to make sense of all the confusion, knowing just what he wanted — to anoint Hubert — and patiently explaining, 'Look, all I shall do is just put oil on his forehead and say a prayer.'" And so, by knowing what he wanted to do and sticking to it, Waugh concludes, the priest finally prevailed: "Hubert crossed himself, . . . so he accepted it" (13 October 1943).

Nonetheless, a real-life incident is one thing and a convincing scene in a novel is another. In his attempt to portray the workings of grace plausibly, Waugh drops hints as to why Alex might have returned to his faith. Alex's very return to Brideshead to die following the death of his wife, after living abroad for years in adultery, implies he has discarded his old hatreds. Another hint is the doctor's comment to Charles about Alex's great fear of death while Alex is undergoing his last illness; this fear may imply that the old man is feeling the stirrings of conscience which finally lead to his act of repentance.

Julia also seems unable to discard her religious faith completely, even though in the course of the story she does give it up to marry a divorced man. Julia, a minor character in the early chapters of the novel, comes to the foreground as the story progresses. During the period of Charles's friendship with Sebastian and marriage to Celia Mulcaster, Julia had fallen in love with a rather gauche Canadian immigrant, Rex Mottram. A crisis arises when Bridey discovers that Rex was divorced six years earlier. Lady Marchmain of course will not hear of Julia's marrying a divorced man.

Julia feels it unfair that the Catholic church should impose burdens and obligations which other religions do not: "If she apostatized now, having been brought up in the Church, she would go to hell, while the Protestant girls of her acquaintance, schooled in happy ignorance, could marry eldest sons, live at peace with their world, and get to heaven before her." But the "gentle old Jesuit" at Farm Street to whom Julia brings her problem is unyielding in his insistence that she give Rex up. From that moment on Julia shuts her mind against her religion. She marries Rex in a dreary nonsectarian ceremony with only a few people present.

Rex proves unfaithful after he and Julia are married only a few months. By this time Charles has found his own wife to have been unfaithful to him. Consequently, when Charles and Julia — who have not seen each other for years — meet by chance, they fall in love with few scruples. They plan to marry when both of their divorces are final.

That Julia is still very sensitive about her religion becomes abundantly clear in her hysterical outburst when Bridey refuses to bring his fiancée, the widow Beryl Muspratt, to Brideshead because Julia is "living in sin" there with Charles. Beryl, Bridey explains, is a woman of "strict Catholic principle fortified by the prejudices of the middle class." Waugh shortened Julia's long, impassioned speech about "living in sin" in the revised version of the novel since, he says in the preface, he felt it somewhat out of keeping with the verisimilitude at which the novel as a whole aims. I reproduce some of it here in order to give its flavor, indicating by brackets a part which Waugh cut in the revised version:

> "*Living in sin*, with sin, [by sin, for sin, every hour, every day, year in year out. Waking up with sin in the morning, seeing the curtains drawn on sin, bathing it, dressing it, clipping diamonds to it, feeding it, showing it round, giving it a good time, putting it to sleep at night with a tablet of Dial if it's fretful.] . . . Mummy dying with it; Christ dying with it, nailed hand and foot; hanging over the bed in the night nursery; . . . hanging in the dark church."

When Charles tells Julia that she has allowed herself to get upset about a lot of nonsense which Nanny Hawkins taught her in the nursery, Julia replies as Sebastian had years before: "How I wish it was." Tension between them begins to build when Julia insists that Alex see a priest before he dies. Charles somehow senses that if Julia reaffirms her religion to this extent she may return to it completely and give him up. Charles's fears prove well grounded. After her father dies reconciled to the Church, Julia tells Charles that they cannot marry.

Scenes such as the one in which Julia gives Charles up to return to the practice of the faith moved some critics to call *Brideshead Revisited* a "Catholic tract." But Waugh is not trying to make the reader accept Julia's reasoning; he is only trying to indicate that Julia's motives, given her background, are convincing. As critic Eric Linklater explains her decision: "She has no illusions about herself; she knows that she is unlikely to live a wholly virtuous life; but within the Church sin may be pardoned, whereas in marriage beyond the Church's recognition she would be outcast, and grace could not reach her."[50]

Waugh has also taken pains throughout the novel to show that Charles's religious conversion is plausible. He has indicated the steps by which Charles has been led to accept the faith, most notably the impact of the regeneration of the three Marchmains on him.

Julia had said that her reunion with Charles after both had

gone their separate ways for years was "part of a plan." In retrospect Charles gradually comes to see how this plan has worked out in his life. He realizes, for instance, that his friendship with Sebastian was the forerunner of his love for Julia. During his love affair with Julia, as Charles puts it, Sebastian was "with me daily in Julia; or rather it was Julia I had known in him in those distant Arcadian days."

Waugh even emphasized the physical resemblance of Sebastian and Julia in lines which he deleted from the page proofs: "So far as women and men can share identity, it was shared by brother and sister; only her sex, embodied in her finer bone and softer skin, distinguished her from my friend." When Charles points out to Julia how much she reminds him of Sebastian, she replies that perhaps she is only a forerunner too, and Charles expands on Julia's remark in his own thoughts:

> "Perhaps . . . all our loves are merely hints and symbols; . . . perhaps you and I are types and this sadness which sometimes falls between us springs from disappointment in our search, each straining through and beyond the other, snatching a glimpse now and then of the shadow which turns the corner always a pace or two ahead of us."

Charles has been unaware that his love first for Sebastian and then for Julia has been leading him on to a higher love. Thus he finds himself, almost in spite of himself, actually kneeling beside Julia at Alex's deathbed and praying for her father, if only for the sake of the woman he loves: "O God, if there is a God, forgive him his sins, if there is such a thing as sin." Charles feels as relieved as the others when Alex makes the sign of the cross to express his repentance.

Then Julia tells Charles what he already knows by this time, that she believes she must give him up. Charles answers, "I hope that your heart may break; but I do understand." The fact that Charles understands Julia's motivation signals that he also has felt the tug of "the twitch upon the thread." This phrase, which serves as the title of the last major section of the book, refers to a line from one of G. K. Chesterton's Father Brown stories. Cordelia says she has been sure all along that God would reclaim the straying members of her family. She then asks, "I wonder if you remember the story mummy read us the evening Sebastian first got drunk. . . . Father Brown said something like 'I caught him' (the thief) 'with an unseen hook and an invisible line which is long enough to let him wander to the ends of the world and still to bring him back with a twitch upon the thread.'"

And so in the epilogue Charles is left where he was in the prologue, an army officer revisiting the Brideshead estate where he had lived such an important phase of his life. And the hint of the prologue is now certain: due to his experiences with the Marchmain family, Charles has become a Catholic himself, despite the fact that most of the Marchmains were less than edifying practitioners of the faith. That hint occurs in the prologue when Hooper, one of Charles's subordinates, tells Charles that he had blundered into the chapel at Brideshead while mass was being offered. "I felt very awkward," Hooper says, "More in your line than mine."

The chapel, a wedding present from Alex to his wife, had been closed after her death. Cordelia had described the event to Charles: the priest "blew out the lamp in the sanctuary and left the tabernacle open and empty, as though from now on it was always to be Good Friday." Now, with the coming of the troops to Brideshead, the chapel has been reopened and a "surprising lot use it, too," observes the quartering commandant to Charles in the epilogue. Charles goes to the chapel and says a prayer, "an ancient, newly learned form of words," thus indicating his recent conversion to Catholicism. As he leaves the chapel, Charles reflects that the builders of Brideshead did not know to what uses their mansion would be put in the centuries to follow:

> "Something quite remote from anything the builders intended has come out of their work, and out of the fierce little human tragedy in which I played; something none of us thought about at the time; a small red flame — a beaten-copper lamp of deplorable design re-

lit before the beaten-copper doors of a tabernacle; the flame which the old knights saw from their tombs, which they saw put out; that flame burns again for other soldiers, far from home. . . . It could not have been lit but for the builders and the tragedians, and there I found it this morning, burning anew among the old stones."

The light of faith continues to burn at Brideshead and unites Charles with the Marchmain family, scattered as they are by the war. On this note the novel ends.

As I pointed out earlier, if Charles Ryder's conversion is to strike the reader as a convincing depiction of human experience, it must be deeply rooted in the psychology of his character. It must seem the plausible outcome of the way his character has developed in the course of the novel. I believe *Brideshead Revisited* stands up under this test.

Waugh has been careful to show the reader that Charles's conversion results from the cumulative effect of the reconciliations with God which he witnessed in Sebastian, in Lord Alex, and finally in Julia. As the critic John Hardy summarizes the chain of events:

> Charles is, in effect, disowned by his father. He is, then, prospectively adopted by Lord Marchmain, apparently as a kind of surrogate for the lost Sebastian, and promised the estate as his inheritance if, as then supposed, he is to marry Julia. And, finally, giving up the inheritance along with Julia, he is ultimately inspired by old Marchmain's deathbed repentance to his own conversion — thus receiving the eternal inheritance, of course, instead of the temporal, and recognition as son of God the Father.[51]

Other critics, however, often object that *Brideshead Revisited* gives a rather negative impression of Waugh's chosen religion. Charles may have gained the faith, but he seems bereft of just about everything else. He describes himself to Hooper as "homeless, childless, middle-aged, and loveless." Has his conversion not cost him too much? "Even I, who happen to be a Catholic," says the Irish author Sean O'Faolain, "fail to see the appeal of any such religion as is here depicted, if for no other reason than that it has brought the minimum of happiness to the maximum number of people; and I do not speak of happiness in the worldly sense."[52]

This same objection was raised by the reader who wrote to Waugh, "Your *Brideshead Revisited* is a strange way to show that Catholicism is an answer to anything. Seems more like the kiss of Death." Waugh dismissed this comment in his *Life* article "Fanfare" by asking facetiously whether "the kiss of Death" had anything to do with halitosis. I myself feel that only religion as Waugh presents it in *Brideshead* could ultimately comfort this group of characters, who — because of their own failings as well as the troubled times — have suffered a great deal of misfortune. Indeed the conclusion of the novel implies, just as Waugh said it would in his "Warning" in the first British edition, that if the human spirit is fortified by faith it can survive all disasters.

This is not to say that *Brideshead* is an apology for the Roman Catholic faith, as some critics have maintained. Surely Waugh has not tried to present Catholicism to his readers in an appealing way calculated to bring them into the Catholic church. Waugh himself has said, "In *Brideshead Revisited* I was not trying to show what life was like in the 'bosom of the Church.' I don't deny that such a novel could be written, but it isn't what I wanted to do."[53]

Indeed in *Commonweal* Waugh once criticized Catholics "who think it the function of the Catholic writer to produce only advertising brochures setting out in attractive terms the advantages of church membership" (16 July 1948). Waugh's friend and fellow writer Christopher Hollis supports his claim that *Brideshead* is not a work of apologetics, i.e., a defense of the Roman Catholic church:

> There is no consideration of the historical and metaphysical evidence for the Catholic claims. A reader who had considered that evidence and rejected it would find nothing in the work to alter his rejection. . . . It is for the apologist to give reasons and to defend the truth of the Church's claims. All that Mr. Waugh, the novelist, is concerned to do is to show the strength of those claims on those who have ever come under their influence.[54]

"It is true," says Father D'Arcy, "that Evelyn wanted to make converts all of his life, but by personal contact, not through his fiction. He had no specific lesson to preach in his novels; he was an artist; he wrote what was in him." As an artist Waugh sought to incorporate thematic implications subtly, without being didactic. He did this by infusing the whole structure and atmosphere of the novel with a religious tone that can be found not only in plot and character but in imagery as well. One such image, perhaps the subtlest religious resonance in the entire novel, is that of the fountain gracing the lawn of the Brideshead estate. The fountain imagery is final evidence of Waugh's consummate artistry and control of his material.

When Charles first sees the fountain he describes it as being "such a fountain as one might expect to find in a piazza of Southern Italy; such a fountain as was, indeed, found there a century ago by one of Sebastian's ancestors; found, purchased, imported and re-erected in an alien but welcoming climate." The fountain is an example of the seventeenth-century Italian baroque artistry that represents for Waugh the Roman Catholic tradition, alien to England after Elizabethan times but nonetheless welcome at Brideshead, where the ancient faith has been preserved intact.

"For me the beauty was new found," comments Charles, for he is gradually becoming interested in the Catholic heritage which the fountain represents. He accordingly sketches the fountain and gives the drawing to Nanny Hawkins, the elderly governess who raised the Marchmain children and who, more than anyone else at Brideshead, has preserved that heritage within herself. Charles sits by the hour contemplating the fountain, "probing its shadows, tracing its lingering echoes, rejoicing in its clustered feats of daring and invention," and while doing so feels "a whole new system of nerves" alive within him, "as though the water that spurted and bubbled among its stones was indeed a life-giving spring."

It is in the chapter entitled "The Fountain" that Charles and

Julia stand by the fountain and discuss her hysterical outburst of religious scruples about marrying Charles, which occurred earlier that evening. The following evening they again hear "the music of the fountain" as a reminder of the Catholic tradition that lies deep within Julia and is becoming meaningful for Charles as well.

Small wonder that, as Hooper reports to Charles in the epilogue, the fountain has been rather a touchy subject with "the landlady" of Brideshead (Julia). Hooper tells him:

> "The young officers used to lark about in it on guest nights and it was looking a bit the worse for wear, so I wired it in and turned the water off. Looks a bit untidy now; all the drivers throw their cigarette-ends and the remains of the sandwiches there, and you can't get to it to clean it up, since I put the wire round it. Florid great thing, isn't it?"

What Charles had called the "life-giving" waters of the fountain have been turned off, significantly by Hooper, whom Waugh has established as a representative of the modern age — an age out of touch with the tradition the fountain represents. This would indeed be a somber note on which to end the novel, and so Waugh balances the final image of the fountain with that of the sanctuary lamp. Its rekindled flame heartens Charles, who feels it indicates that the flame of faith will continue to burn in him, and in those who were part of his life at Brideshead.

Waugh does picture Charles as homeless, childless, and loveless at the end of the novel, rather like Tony Last at the end of *A Handful of Dust*. But unlike Tony, Charles has found meaning in his suffering through faith now that he has come "to accept the supernatural as the real." What Cordelia once said of Sebastian now seems to apply to Charles as well: "No one is ever holy without suffering. . . . It's the spring of love." Thus Charles has gone a significant step beyond the heroes of Waugh's earlier satirical fiction in having achieved spiritual growth through misfortune.

One cannot doubt, then, that Waugh tried throughout this novel to depict a whole human, including that human's determining character of being "God's creature with a defined purpose." As Waugh promised emphatically in his *Life* essay of 1946, he would continue this attempt in his subsequent serious fiction.

The method Waugh used to introduce his personal religious vision into the fiction that follows *Brideshead* varies from book to book. There is the cartoon-like caricature of an upcoming pagan generation which he drew in *Love among the Ruins;* the more straight forward religious portrait of a fourth-century saint in *Helena;* and, best of all, *The Loved One,* in which Waugh lampooned the false glamour and materialism of our age as epitomized in Hollywood and Forest Lawn Cemetery. More than *Love among the Ruins* or *Helena, The Loved One* is a product of Waugh's immediate experience — in this case a trip to California which he made in 1947. The book underscores once more that Waugh was at his best writing about things he knew firsthand. Now on with Waugh to Hollywood.

5

The Loved One among the Ruins: The Later Fiction

After the war Waugh settled down to a life resembling that of an English country squire at Piers Court in Gloucestershire. "By that time," says Harriet Waugh of her father, "he was older and more serious. He no longer lived in London society, which had served as the setting for his earlier fiction, although he still went up to London to visit old friends. He had become a sadder man." By living in semi-seclusion, Waugh seemed to be underlining his conviction that the modern world was decaying into an age of barbarism in which

> vice no longer pays lip service to virtue. The artist's only service to the disintegrated society of today is to create little independent systems of order of his own. I foresee in the dark age opening that the scribes may play the part of the monks after the first barbarian victories. (Life, 8 April 1946)

Some might have thought that Waugh spoke tongue in cheek when expressing his respect for monasticism and comparing the role of writer in the modern age to that of a medieval monk who helps preserve Christian civilization. Yet from all indications he was deeply serious. He made a trip to the Trappist monastery at Gethsemani, Kentucky, to talk with Thomas Merton, who later wrote in a letter to Waugh scholar Paul A. Doyle that Waugh was very taken with monastic life: "One thing that had especially amused him in *The Seven Storey Mountain* was the bit about the monks out in the woods chopping trees and saying 'All for Jesus' at each blow of the axe. He gave an energetic imitation of what he thought this was like" (5 June 1968).

In a more serious vein Waugh remarked in *Commonweal* that monasticism was a subject which he had at heart "because I believe that we are returning to a stage when on the supernatural plane only heroic prayer can save us, and when on the natural plane the cloister offers a saner and more civilized life than 'the world'" (11 March 1949). Significantly Tony, nephew of the hero of Waugh's war trilogy, becomes a monk when he is released from the service. When Waugh was accused of being a reactionary for holding such views as those just indicated, he replied, "An artist must be a reactionary. He has to stand out against the tenor of the age and not go flopping along; he must offer some little opposition. Even the great Victorian artists were all anti-Victorian, despite the pressures to conform."[55]

Included in Waugh's later fiction, after *Brideshead Revisited* but before the *Sword of Honor* trilogy, are three works which taken together form a kind of minor trilogy, a prelude to the war trilogy. All three of the works deal with the relation of Christianity to a pagan milieu. *The Loved One* is a satire aimed at the decline of religious belief and practice in the twentieth century, as evidenced in the California burial customs Waugh had observed while in Hollywood. *The Loved One* shows Christianity losing its foothold in modern society. In *Helena* Waugh reaches back to the fourth century to show Christianity striving to gain a foothold in the empire of pagan Rome. In *Love among the Ruins* Waugh projects into the future to show the post-Christian world toward which man was headed in *The Loved One*.

The Loved One (1948)

The story of how Waugh came to write *The Loved One* provides an interesting background for the reading of the novel. Because of the great popularity of *Brideshead Revisited*, Waugh was invited to Hollywood in 1947 by Metro-Goldwyn-Mayer to discuss the possibility of filming it. He accepted the invitation ruefully because he had always been suspicious of attempts to adapt his fiction to stage or screen. Ten years earlier, for example, Waugh had curtly discouraged Irving Wallace (now a novelist himself) from dramatizing *A Handful of Dust*. In November 1936 Waugh responded to Wallace in a letter which is, characteristically, undated, and which Mr. Wallace has kindly shared with me. "I am of course unable to authorize any version until I have seen it," said Waugh, "and I should not authorize any version which made considerable changes in the action or dialogue. I will consider any version you care to send me, but I think it is fair to warn you that I am not favorably predisposed to the idea of its being dramatized."

Almost inevitably, given Waugh's attitude toward adaptations, after several weeks of dickering over changes in the story of *Brideshead*, Waugh refused MGM's offer of $150,000 for the screen rights. "Each of the books purchased by a studio," Waugh later commented acidly, "has had some individual quality, good or bad, that has made it remarkable. It is the work of a staff of 'writers' to distinguish this quality, separate it, and obliterate it."[56] The chief screenwriter assigned to adapt *Brideshead* was an English expatriate who was to appear in *The Loved One* as Sir Francis Hinsley; he saw *Brideshead* purely as a love story. "None of them see the theological implication," Waugh wrote in his diary about the studio people with whom he was dealing (7 February 1947). The producer "lost heart as soon as I explained to him what *Brideshead* was about," Waugh added later, and in the end the producer used the censor's objections to some aspects of the plot as an easy way out of the project. The film was cancelled, much to Waugh's relief.

But like Dennis Barlow, hero of *The Loved One*, Waugh took home with him to England "a great chunk of experience, the artist's load," for he had garnered enough material while in Hollywood to write *The Loved One*.

In his preface to the novel in the Second Uniform Edition, Waugh recalls that "the awful inefficiency of studio and hotel" might have ruined his stay in Los Angeles had he not discovered "the unsurpassed glories" of Forest Lawn, the cemetery he calls "Whispering Glades" in his novel. "A large car came daily to take me to the studio; daily I directed it to the graveyard where I spent long periods of delight penetrating the arcana of that lustrous trade." Indeed Waugh felt that cemeteries were the only real thing he had encountered in Hollywood. "I found a deep mine of literary gold in the cemetery of Forest Lawn," says Waugh in rounding off his diary account of his Hollywood sojourn," and intend to get to work immediately on a novelette staged there" (7 April 1947).

Waugh thus joined the ranks of distinguished novelists who have embodied their unhappy experiences with Hollywood in their fiction, notably Nathaniel West in *Day of the Locust*, F. Scott Fitzgerald in *The Last Tycoon* and the Pat Hobby stories, and Norman Mailer in *The Deer Park*.

Waugh felt that during his visit he had antagonized the English "colony" in Hollywood, who were very defensive about living there permanently; but his remorse was only momentary, for he went on to caricature their situation in *The Loved One*. The first scene of the story introduces one of the English "colony" in Hollywood who, like his colleagues, has sold his talents (and his soul, Waugh implies) to the film capital. Sir Francis Hinsley came to Hollywood as a respected scriptwriter but has been demoted to the publicity department. Waugh's description of Sir Francis's home and its environs carries the reader back to the jungles of *Black Mischief* and *A Handful of Dust*. One notices the insuperable heat and the ever-present pulse of music from neighboring "huts" as Sir Francis chats with Dennis, newly arrived from England, about Dennis's prospects for a successful career in Holly-wood. They are "the counterparts of numberless fellow-countrymen exiled in the barbarous regions of the world."

Dennis, at twenty-eight, is full of ambition. Sir Francis warns him not to fall under the dehumanizing influences of the Holly-wood dream factory, as Sir Francis himself and so many others have: "The studios keep us going with a pump. We are still just capable of a few crude reactions — nothing more. If we ever got disconnected from our bottle, we should simply crumble." Sir Francis's remark that he is Dennis's *memento mori* ("reminder of death") proves to be literally true. When Sir Francis is peremp-torily fired by the studio, having outlived his usefulness, he goes home and hangs himself. Thus Waugh introduces the novel's preoccupation with death.

In an article for *Life* magazine called "Death in Hollywood," which Waugh wrote as a warm-up for *The Loved One,* Waugh spoke of the has-beens he had seen around Hollywood. They probably suggested to him aspects of the character of Sir Fran-cis: "Death is the only event which can now disturb them, and priests of countless preposterous cults have gathered round to shade off that change until it becomes imperceptible," he wrote (29 September 1947). When Dennis visits Whispering Glades to arrange for Sir Francis's funeral, he is interested in seeing how the cult of death is practiced there, partly because by this time he has gotten a job at the Happier Hunting Ground, a pet cemetery, in lieu of launching a career in films. And so it is as "a missionary priest, making his first pilgrimage to the Vatican" that Dennis goes to Whispering Glades for the first time.

Waugh based Whispering Glades on Forest Lawn Memorial Park in Los Angeles, which he likened to a "necropolis of the age of the Pharaohs." Skeptics who suspect Waugh of exaggerating in his depictions of Forest Lawn in the *Loved One* need only visit the cemetery, as I did recently, to see that such is not the case. How closely Whispering Glades is patterned on Forest Lawn is exemplified by the fact that Waugh used the "credo" of the late

Dr. Hubert Eaton, founder of Forest Lawn, as the basis for the inscription which confronts Dennis as he enters Whispering Glades:

> Behold I dreamed a dream and I saw a New Earth sacred to HAPPINESS. There amid all that Nature and Art could offer to elevate the Soul of Man I saw the Happy Resting Place of Countless Loved Ones. And I saw the Waiting Ones who still stood at the brink of that narrow stream that now separated them from those who had gone before. Young and old they were happy too. Happy . . . in the certain knowledge that their Loved Ones were very near, in Beauty and Happiness such as the earth cannot give. . . .
>
> Wilbur Kenworthy, The Dreamer

Dr. Eaton's own statement reads in part, "I believe in a happy Eternal Life. I believe those of us left behind should be glad in the certain belief that those gone before have entered into that happier Life." The implication of this and other texts which Waugh observed at Forest Lawn clearly signified to him that "Forest Lawn has consciously turned its back on the 'old customs of Death,' the grim traditional alternatives of Heaven and Hell, and promises immediate eternal happiness for all its inmates. . . . Dr. Eaton is the first man to offer eternal salvation at an inclusive charge as part of his undertaking service."

For Waugh this attitude toward death is symptomatic of a basic tendency in contemporary civilization to exalt the material and ignore the spiritual. It is this more fundamental attitude that Waugh satirizes in the novel when, for example, one of the attendants at Whispering Glades tells Dennis that Dr. Kenworthy "does not approve of wreaths or crosses." Waugh had noticed the absence of religious symbols at Forest Lawn; he remarked in his *Life* article of 1947 that a Christian visitor might reflect that, in contrast, "by far the commonest feature of other graveyards is still the Cross, a symbol in which previous generations have found more Life and Hope than in the most elaborately watered evergreen shrub." Such reflections are not made explicit in the novel, where Waugh allows the reader to infer the implications of the satire for himself.

Thus Waugh the novelist does not comment in *The Loved One* on the fact that Mr. Joyboy, the eccentric chief mortician at Whispering Glades, folds Sir Francis's hands in a gesture not of prayer but of resignation. Robert Murray Davis, in a study of the novel's text, mentions that Waugh brought back from America a copy of Ray Slocum's *Embalming Techniques* to help him with the technical details of this and other scenes in the story. Slocum's chapter on hanging undoubtedly underlies Waugh's description of Joyboy's treatment of Sir Francis's corpse, for it details the method of dealing with just the kind of facial discoloration and distortion apparent on Sir Francis's dead countenance.[57]

Since liturgy in Hollywood "is the concern of the Stage rather than of the Clergy," no one minds when Dennis composes a poem to read at the burial service for Sir Francis. Dennis's grotesque apostrophe to the dead knight concludes:

> . . . now 'tis here you lie;
> Here pickled in formaldehyde and painted like a
> whore,
> Shrimp-pink incorruptible, not lost nor gone before.

Dennis's poem aptly expresses the sentiments of Dr. Kenworthy's plaque at the entrance to Whispering Glades.

During the course of his visits to Whispering Glades to arrange for Sir Francis's funeral, Dennis meets and falls in love with Aimée Thanatogenos, an assistant mortician there. Aimée's last name means, in Greek, "child of death." Hence she seems to have been fated to work at Whispering Glades. Her first name was given to her by her father in honor of the American evangelist Aimée Semple McPherson, whom Waugh had already satirized in the character of Mrs. Melrose Ape in *Vile Bodies.* Aimée's father, it seems, was a strong adherent of the "Four Square Gospel" cult and therefore an admirer of Miss McPherson.

Unlike Dennis, Aimée has a very definite creed by which she lives, due to her upbringing: "I am progressive and therefore have no religion but I do not think religion is a thing to be cynical about because it makes some people very happy and all cannot be progressive at this stage of Evolution." Aimée is an example of one who adheres to Christian morality without understanding the principles that underlie it. Yet she does have a substitute for religion in her life: Whispering Glades.

As Dennis points out to Aimée, her work at the cemetery has in fact become her religion. Furthermore he reminds Aimée that she has sworn to love him eternally "with the most sacred oath in the religion of Whispering Glades." In short, Dennis thinks of Aimée as "the sole Eve in a bustling hygienic Eden." Paul Pennyfeather, Tony Last, and some of Waugh's other early heroes may have been unhappy as exiles from Eden; Aimée is content to let Whispering Glades be her paradise. She looks upon its insulated atmosphere as her protection against the harsh realities of the outside world.

Nevertheless, when she cannot decide whether to marry Joyboy or Dennis (she does not yet know that Dennis works in a pet cemetery), Aimée seeks spiritual advice outside Whispering Glades. She has recourse to the Guru Brahmin, whose column appears daily in a local newspaper. Her letters are actually answered by Mr. Slump, who lives in an ever-increasing alcoholic haze. Slump becomes irritated when Aimée is not satisfied with the standard advice he dispenses and is particularly disgruntled when she phones him at a bar, after he has been fired, in order to get one last helping of wisdom. Aimée has just found to her horror that Dennis works at Happier Hunting Ground. She asks Slump if she should therefore break her engagement. In exasperation Slump advises her to take the elevator to the top floor of whatever building she happens to be in, to find "a nice window and jump out."

Because Aimée has placed all her confidence in her Guru, she follows Slump's advice and takes her life. She goes to Joyboy's workroom on the top floor of the mortuary and takes cyanide. Living constantly in an atmosphere of death, Aimée has never learned to cope with life; she goes to join the dead among whom she has learned to feel at home.

Dennis, on the other hand, has learned to thrive in the world that has crushed Aimée. He has never taken the rituals of Whispering Glades as seriously as Aimée has. Aimée once described Dennis in a letter to the Guru Brahmin as being "cynical at things which should be sacred. I do not think he has any religion." But Dennis does become interested in religion after talking to the nonsectarian clergyman Reverend Bartholomew, whose burial rites at the Happier Hunting Ground feature such inspiring sermons as the one that begins, "Dog that is born of bitch hath but a short time to live."

Dennis's initial idea is to become a nonsectarian minister in order to impress Aimée. Reverend Bartholomew assures him that a nonsectarian clergyman is the social equal of an embalmer like Mr. Joyboy because "there is a deep respect in the American heart for ministers of religion." Dennis accordingly has a card printed to announce his new profession:

> Squadron Leader the Rev. Dennis Barlow begs to announce that he is shortly starting business at 1154 Arbuckle Avenue, Los Angeles. All nonsectarian services expeditiously conducted at competitive prices. Funerals a specialty.

And so Dennis for a time joins Waugh's assortment of eccentric if not always bogus spiritual advisors: Mr. Prendergast, the Modern Churchman of *Decline and Fall;* Reverend Tendril, the benighted vicar of Tony Last's parish in *A Handful of Dust;* and Mr. Slump, the Guru Brahmin of *The Loved One.*

Once Aimée has committed suicide, Dennis decides to relinquish his call to the ministry in favor of blackmailing Mr. Joyboy, who fears that Aimée's death will bring scandal to himself and to Whispering Glades. Dennis offers to incinerate Aimée's body in the pet cemetery's crematorium and let it be thought that Aimée has gone to England with him, provided Joyboy pays his first-class passage home. Joyboy agrees and Dennis sets about arranging "his loved one's final combustion." The reduction of the human spirit to the level of that of other animals, implied from the start by the existence of the Happier Hunting Ground, is completed when Dennis arranges to have a card sent to Mr. Joy-boy annually from the pet cemetery on the anniversary of Aimée's death: "Your little Aimée is wagging her tail in heaven tonight, thinking of you."

Edmund Wilson resented the religious implications of *The Loved One* just as much as he had those he found in *Brideshead Revisited*: "To the nonreligious reader, . . . the patrons and proprietors of Whispering Glades seem more sensible and less absurd than the priest-guided Evelyn Waugh."[58] Wilson was quite right in thinking that beneath the satire in *The Loved One* are Waugh's own religious convictions, acting as the norms supporting the satire. As Waugh himself put it:

> What I found disagreeable about modern burial customs in their more extravagant form was the implied suggestion that *all* one owed to the dead was a splendid funeral and grave. That there was no need to pray for the repose of their souls if their bodies reposed in pretty spaces. Some of the advertising seemed to guarantee eternal felicity to all buried in their precincts. And the pets' cemeteries seemed to blur the distinction between animal and human life.[59]

Others have felt that Waugh was giving a one-sided picture of America as totally materialistic by reducing the country to the eccentricities of Hollywood and Forest Lawn. Waugh's intention as a satirist, however, was rather to use Hollywood and Forest Lawn as symptoms of a materialistic strain in modern society as a whole, not only in America. But on more than one occasion Waugh expressed his respect for American life. He admired what he called the "positively tangible quality to the faith in America." Once, in New Orleans, for example, he noticed that on Ash Wednesday the Jesuit Church facing his hotel was busy all day; there Catholics were having the sign of the cross made on their foreheads with ashes while "the old grim message was being repeated over each penitent: 'Dust thou art and unto dust thou shalt return.' . . . Here it was, plainly stated, plainly accepted, and all that day, all over that light-hearted city, one encountered the little black smudge on the forehead which sealed us members of a great brotherhood who can rejoice and recognize the limits of rejoicing."

Waugh found Christianity and "pre-eminently Catholicism" to be the "redeeming part" of the American pursuit of the good life. Travel in America, he discovered, would dispose of the European and Asiatic notion that "Americanism" meant materialism and spiritual poverty: "There is a purely American 'way of life' led by every good American Christian that is point-for-point opposed to the publicized and largely fictitious 'way of life' dreaded in Europe and Asia. And that, by the grace of God, is the 'way of life' that will prevail."[60] It was from this frame of reference, then, that Waugh wrote *The Loved One* and described what he saw as departures from the true spirit of Christian life which he had found in America.

Since *The Loved One* is about Hollywood, it is fitting that Hollywood should want to film it; and the film version in its own way increases one's appreciation of *The Loved One*. MGM undertook the project in 1964. Onlookers conjectured that the film company would get no further in its attempt to film *The Loved One* than it had in its attempt to film *Brideshead Revisited*. To everyone's surprise Waugh agreed to let the filming proceed.

"He had initially turned *The Loved One* over to his very good friend Alec Guinness, who was going to star in the film for an independent producer," Mrs. Waugh explained to me. "When the latter went bankrupt, however, the script was turned over, along with some other properties, to MGM, who proceeded with the film."

Guinness then proved unavailable, and when the director, Tony Richardson, announced the extent of the changes he wanted made in *The Loved One* to "update" it, Waugh demanded that the director be replaced. But Waugh's objections came too late; the film went into production according to Richardson's specifications. The "expansion" of the script got decidedly out of hand, admits sick humorist Terry Southern, one of the collaborators on the screenplay. The first assembly of the footage after principal photography had been completed ran to five hours and had to be trimmed to two.[61] In the course of all these revisions, Waugh's original story got mislaid, as he had feared it would be. "He tried to have his name removed from the screen credits," said Mrs. Waugh, "but it was already too late to do so."

The finished product opened in London only two weeks before Waugh's death in the spring of 1966. He would never have gone to see it in any case. Most of the reviews of the film were ultimately tributes to Waugh since they pointed out how his superb satire had been debased by the film's bad taste. *Newsweek*'s review is typical:

> In place of the beautifully controlled satiric explosion that Waugh's little volume visited upon an unsuspecting public in 1948, Richardson's blowsy film relies on scatter-gun gagsmanship, much of it derivative, and on camp, some of it dirty. . . . Isn't satire supposed to be offensive? . . . Of course. The crucial difference is that the film version of *The Loved One* fails at satire and therefore never earns the right to be scabrous. (18 October 1965)

Waugh's novel succeeds as satire where the film based so loosely on it fails because Waugh's religious vision provides a climate in which the outrageous behavior of his characters becomes thought-provoking as well as absurd. Lacking any frame of reference at all, the film fails even to be funny, which the book certainly is. If Waugh's novel were not so funny, notes Graham Greene in his review of the book, "how revolting it would be. The grotesque details are pressed firmly, relentlessly, home by Mr. Waugh's thumb like sand in a child's pail."

Greene furthermore compliments Waugh the satirist for being right on target with his humorous barbs and by no means guilty of exaggeration. "It is only a few weeks ago," says Greene, writing in late 1948, "that a famous film star [Carole Landis] was buried at Forest Lawn and the pall bearers were stopped for autographs and interviews, and Mr. Pat O'Brien, a film actor, told the Press, 'This is the hardest matinee that Carole and I have ever played together.' . . . No, Mr. Waugh's world is as near to ours as the country of the Yahoos," one of the nasty places Gulliver visits in Swift's *Gulliver's Travels*.[62]

"In upholding the dignity of death Mr. Waugh is emphasizing the dignity of man," critic Patricia Corr writes. "Suffering, pain, and death are bitter pills in an era whose concern is material progress and comfortable living, and these are the pills which Mr. Waugh prescribes in *The Loved One*."[63] In sum, *The Loved One* ranks with the best of Waugh's satires. Indeed, he never again wrote such a successfully sustained piece of satire.

Helena (1950)

In his next novel, *Helena,* Waugh decided to fictionalize the life of Helena, a fourth-century saint. He wanted to show Christianity gaining ground in the pagan Roman empire, just as he had shown Christianity losing ground in the contemporary world of *The Loved One. Helena* was, furthermore, part of a plan of several novels which Waugh had conceived on a side trip he made to the Holy Land in 1935 while assigned as a war correspondent to Abyssinia:

> So elated was I by the beauties about me that I there and then began vaguely planning a series of books — semi-historic, semi-poetic fiction, I did not quite know what — about the long, intricate, intimate relations between England and the Holy Places. The list of great and strange Britons who from time to time embodied the association — Helena, Richard Lionheart, Stratford Canning, Gordon — would without doubt grow with research. Helena above all first began a ferment in my imagination which lasted for fifteen years. I completed a novel about her which failed in most cases to communicate my enthusiasm.[64]

Waugh began writing *Helena* in the spring of 1945, his diary states, just as World War II drew to a close in Europe: "I thank God to find myself still a writer and at work on something as 'uncontemporary' as I am," he reflected (7 May 1945). He worked on it off and on for some years, interrupting its composition to write *The Loved One,* among other things. It was finally published in 1950. Waugh's enthusiasm for his projected series of novels on the Holy Land never faltered, but he abandoned it after the cool reception accorded *Helena* by both the critics and the general public.

Waugh sometimes called himself a biographer, says his daughter Teresa. He had in mind his biographies of the Elizabethan Jesuit martyr Edmund Campion and of Msgr. Ronald Knox. Critics often lump *Helena* with those books, but Waugh insists in his original preface to *Helena* that the book is a novel. He had pointed out in his preface to his life of Campion (1935) that he had studiously adhered to the facts, although he had "selected the incidents which strike a novelist as important" and put them into a narrative which he hoped would prove readable. Since little is known about Helena's life, however, Waugh says in his preface, he allowed his imagination wider scope:

> Where the authorities are doubtful, I have often chosen the picturesque in preference to the plausible; I have once or twice, where they are silent, freely invented; but there is nothing, I believe, contrary to authentic history (save for certain willful, obvious anachronisms which are introduced as a literary device), and there is little that has not some support from tradition or from early documents.

One of the anachronistic devices which Waugh employs in the novel is the use of modern colloquial speech, in order to make the historical figures in this tale — his only excursion into historical fiction — more vivid for the modern reader.

The theme of the novel is basically the same as that of *Brideshead Revisited,* "an attempt to trace the workings of Divine purpose in a pagan world." The pagan world of Helena's time was that of the Roman empire, on which Christian civilization had yet to make an impact.

Helena is introduced as a spirited young English girl reminiscent of Cordelia in *Brideshead Revisited.* She too has had a religious upbringing; but she is more interested in adventure and romance than Cordelia ever was. As her tutor reads *The Iliad* of Homer to her, she becomes entranced by the story of the fall of Troy, brought about by Paris's abduction of Helena's namesake, Helen of Troy. Helena tells her tutor that she would like to find the lost city of Troy. But she soon forgets this girlish dream, just as Tony Last relinquished his dream of finding his Lost City in *A Handful of Dust.* When she marries the Roman officer Constantius Chlorus, she conceives a desire to see *the* city of the pagan world: Rome.

After their marriage, Constantius revives his interest in the cult of Mithras, the religion of his youth. Helena becomes curious about the cult. But when her husband explains to her the mythology on which the cult is based, she presses him for facts: "And *when* did this happen? How do you know, if no one was there?" Helena will not accept a religion which to its proponents is ineffable but which to her is simply vague and shadowy. She likewise cannot adhere to the Roman state religion, with its innumerable gods and its cult of the emperor, any more than her son Constantine can. Constantine, who will himself be emperor one day, tells her that the empire is being held together by the superstitious allegiance people still feel for "the sanctity of the name of Rome — a bluff two hundred years out of date." Helena then learns from Constantine that the Christians look upon Rome as a holy city for their own reasons: because "the tombs of their first leaders are there."

Helena wants to learn more of Christianity and does so when she meets Lactantius, a fugitive Christian. She is impressed by the clarity with which he speaks of his religion:

> "We have the accounts written by witnesses. Besides that there is the living memory of the Church. We have knowledge handed down from father to son, invisible places marked by memory — the cave where he was born, the tomb where his body was laid, the grave of Peter. One day all these things will be made public. Now they are kept a secret."

Just when Helena feels she is on the brink of learning about a religion that can prove its credentials by citing concrete happenings in time and space, Lactantius disappoints her by refusing to tell her any more because "there are things that must not be spoken of to anyone outside the household." Disconsolate, Helena replies, "All my life I have caused offense to religious people by asking questions."

Yet somehow Helena, like Charles Ryder, becomes convinced of the claims of Christianity and is baptized. Waugh does not describe her conversion or the events leading up to it, though he probably intended the conversation between Helena and Lactantius a few pages earlier in the book to indicate how Helena was being led to baptism. "Was she persuaded point by point," Waugh asks, or did she "lie open unresisting to Divine Grace and so without design become its brimming vehicle? We do not know."

Waugh treated Charles Ryder's conversion in an implicit fashion too, but the method that worked for him in the case of Ryder does not work as well in the case of Helena. Since Ryder's conversion is prefigured through the whole of *Brideshead Revisited,* Waugh can refer to the event indirectly in the epilogue with no loss of impact. But Helena's conversion occurs midway through the novel and is the key to her later behavior. Consequently when Waugh only alludes to it casually, the reader feels he has missed a climax. Historically, no more is known about Helena's conversion than that it occurred. But Waugh the novelist could have supplied the missing details from the resources of his imagination in the same way that he filled other gaps in the narrative.

Helena becomes a changed person as a result of accepting Christianity. Her fellow Christians she looks upon as an intimate family circle, unified with her in the "Mystical Body of Christ, the Church" (a phrase used later by Guy Crouchback's father, in the *Sword of Honor* trilogy). Helena tries to persuade Constantine to be baptized too, but his personal beliefs are an odd mixture of Christianity and paganism. Although he is generally regarded as a Christian because of his Edict of Milan, proclaiming religious toleration for the Christian church, Constantine waits until he is on his deathbed to consider the question of baptism.

Waugh's treatment of Constantine's eclectic religious beliefs echoes his satire of the religious sects depicted in *Black Mischief*, which had the same proclivity for choosing elements congenial to them from both paganism and Christianity. Constantine is the perfect embodiment of this attitude: "The Supreme Deity recognized by Constantine was something far wide of the Christian Trinity. . . . It was all very vague, very plainly designed to please; the lucky thought of a man too busy to worry about niceties or profundities."

In a mood of depression Constantine confides to his mother that he is not really at peace with himself. Helena, at a loss to make him understand her desire that he be baptized, can only tell him that his unhappiness springs from his rule's being one of "Power without Grace." Waugh's friend and critic Christopher Hollis comments on this passage:

> Whether he is dealing with important or with unimportant politicians, whatever the precise extravagances to which they resort, Mr. Waugh's lesson is substantially the same. It is that Power, left to itself, tends to corrupt. He who wields Power can only hope to preserve himself from corruption if . . . he is constantly conscious that he holds it only as the Vice-Regent of God and asks continually for Grace to save him from the natural consequences of Power.[65]

Helena had never been impressed by the trappings of imperial Rome, and that phrase — "Power without Grace" — sums up her attitude. Though she had looked forward to visiting Rome itself someday, she had not been particularly awed years before by the sight of the Roman wall, even though her husband Constantius spoke of it as stretching along the outer reaches of the empire, "a single great girdle round the civilized world." Helena had countered, "Instead of the barbarian breaking in, might The City one day break out? . . . I meant couldn't the wall be at the limits of the world and all men, civilized and barbarian, have a share in The City?"

Constantius was concerned with the survival of Roman civilization within the confines of the empire, the only source of permanence and continuity he knew. Helena even then was thinking of the growth of Roman civilization beyond those boundaries. Little did either of them realize, Waugh implies, in what sense Helena's still half-formed notion would become a reality: that the spread of Christianity would help bring Roman civilization to the world beyond the Roman wall, so that all men, civilized and barbarian alike, could have a share not merely in the City of Man but in the City of God.

Waugh wrote shortly after his conversion to Catholicism, "Civilization — and by this I do not mean talking cinemas and tinned food, nor even surgery and hygienic houses, but the whole moral and artistic organization of Europe — has not in itself the power of survival. It came into being through Christianity, and without it has no significance or power to command allegiance."[66] It is not Roman civilization alone, then, but Roman civilization as informed and preserved by Christianity that Helena comes to see as the basis of western culture in her time. She realizes this when, at the invitation of Constantine, she finally visits Rome for the first time at the age of seventy.

Helena discusses the state of the Church with Pope Sylvester, who agrees that Christianity must extend beyond the boundaries of the empire. He is glad that increased numbers are joining the Church but is concerned about the confusion which theological controversy is causing. An example is the debate about the relationship of Christ's human nature to his divinity, a relationship called by theologians the hypostatic union. Helena, wondering how she can use her prestigious position as Empress Dowager to help the church, is suddenly inspired: she will try to find the relics of the cross on which Christ was crucified. "Just at this moment," she says, "when everyone is forgetting it and chattering about the hypostatic union, there's a solid chunk of wood waiting for them to have their silly heads knocked against. I'm going to find it."

Helena sets out for the Holy Land. Those she questions find themselves confronted not with the gentle, elderly aristocrat they had anticipated, but with "a crank; and more than a crank, a saint." She takes the Three Wise Men as her spiritual patrons because she somehow realizes that she, like them, will live on in one historic act of devotion and because she, like them, was late in coming:

> "Yet you came and were not turned away. You too found room before the manger. . . . Dear cousins, pray for me, . . . and for my poor overloaded son. May he, too, before the end find kneeling space in the straw. Pray for the great, . . . the learned, the oblique, the delicate. Let them not be quite forgotten at the Throne of God when the simple come into their kingdom."

"He thought that prayer one of the best passages that he ever wrote," said Mrs. Waugh. "He felt a particular affinity for Helena at this period of her life because she was trying to cope with the Modern Age of her own time."

When her investigations in Jerusalem apparently come to nothing, Helena takes to her bed on Good Friday night, soothed by a sleeping potion. She has a dream in which the fabled Wandering Jew tells her that she will find the cross in a cistern outside the city gate of Jerusalem, where it was thrown after the Crucifixion. In the preface to *Helena,* Waugh explains that he introduced the Wandering Jew into his narrative as a device for reconciling two discrepant stories of the discovery of the cross: "one, that Helena was led to the spot in a dream; the second and less creditable version, that she extorted the information from an elderly rabbi by putting him down a well and leaving him there for a week."

The Wandering Jew tells Helena that, many years before, he had curtly told Christ to move on when Christ had stumbled and fallen on the doorstep of the Jew's shop on his way to Calvary, and that Christ had told the Jew to tarry until his Second Coming at the end of the world as a penance for what the Jew had said. So the Jew lives on, ostensibly getting no older, plying his trade as an incense merchant. Since he sells at shrines of all religious sects, the Jew is willing to help Helena find the cross for this will eventually mean another shrine for him to service.

> Helena listened and in her mind saw . . . the sanctuaries of Christendom become a fair ground, stalls hung with beads and medals, substances yet unknown pressed into sacred emblems; heard a chatter of haggling in tongues as yet unspoken. . . . She saw all this, considered it and said: "It's a stiff price"; and then: "Show me the Cross."

When Helena awakes she determines to have her workmen dig where the Jew had suggested in her dream. The cross is finally found and identified. She had accomplished her task, and "with her precious cargo . . . she sailed away, out of authentic history."

In Waugh's short story "Period Piece" (1934), the elderly Lady Amelia remarks that women of her age "always devote themselves either to religion or to novels. . . . I have remarked among my few surviving friends that those who read novels enjoy far better health." Obviously Lady Amelia had never heard of Helena, who thought her life was over when her husband divorced her to make a political marriage but accomplished a religious goal that constituted the most important action of her life — all this at an age when most women would have been content to live out their days with their memories.

Waugh developed this theme in an essay, "St. Helena, Empress," which he originally wrote as an introduction for the BBC radio version of his recently published novel. There is only one saint any person can become, Waugh writes, and that is the saint that God intended him or her to be:

> There is only one saint Bridget Hogan can actually become, and that is "St. Bridget Hogan," and that is the saint she must become

. . . if she is to enter heaven. She cannot slip through in fancy-dress, made up as Joan of Arc.

Helena had become the saint that God wanted her to be: St. Helena, Empress; not St. Helena, Martyr, or St. Helena, Anchorite. By accepting throughout her life the normal bereavements and disappointments all have to face, says Waugh, Helena prepared herself to perform a special task when called upon by God to do so, something previously unattempted and unrepeatable, which under the circumstances she alone seemed able to do.

As Waugh sees it, Helena's action thus reflected the divine purpose working in a pagan world. Helena realized that the City of God on earth must have a solid foundation of fact if men were to recognize it and become its citizens. Accordingly she bluntly reasserted that God had become man and died on the cross to redeem mankind. She did this at a time when theological speculation was threatening to refine and diminish this essential fact of the Christian faith until it had lost its meaning. "There is no guarantee which would satisfy the antiquary of the authenticity of Helena's discovery," Waugh admits. "What we can learn from Helena is something about the workings of God; that He wants a different thing from each of us, laborious or easy, conspicuous or quite private, but something which only we can do and for which we were created."[67]

"Evelyn thought *Helena* his most perfect novel," says Reverend Martin D'Arcy, "because his own personal thesis was best put forth in it: that God put man on this earth to do a special task and God took man away only when he had done what God had put him here to do." *Helena* was consequently one of his favorites among his novels — "the only one of his books that he ever cared to read aloud to the whole family," says Harriet Waugh. But although *Helena* best demonstrates Waugh's thesis about man's relationship to God, it is not, artistically speaking, his best novel. It is flawed by two faults which Waugh was always prone to commit in his serious fiction but usually managed to avoid.

The first of these faults is Waugh's tendency to allow minor characters to usurp the stage from the central figures at times simply because of the engaging way in which they are drawn. Anthony Blanche in *Brideshead Revisited* is one example; Apthorpe in the *Sword of Honor* trilogy is another. But only in the case of Constantine in *Helena* does a subordinate character seem to fascinate the author (and therefore the reader) to the point of almost eclipsing the main character.

Helena herself is an uncomplicated, straightforward person who makes important decisions and sticks to them. But Constantine is an intriguing bundle of contradictions who can be comic at one moment and sinister at the next. He gives Christianity official sanction throughout the empire with the Edict of Milan and claims to have won an important battle with divine help; but he refuses to consider baptism until he can receive it on his deathbed and have all of his sins wiped out at once. He kills his grown son at the instigation of his nefarious wife Fausta but later roasts her alive in her bath because she has suggested that he do away with his mother as well. Constantine is at long last baptized and dies in the expectation of "an immediate triumphal entry into Paradise" as befits an emperor.

Perhaps Constantine stands out more than his role in the novel would warrant because his erratic character offers so much scope for Waugh's imagination and wit. Nevertheless, as literary critic James Carens has noted, Helena ultimately retains her central place in the novel because she is the norm by which all the objects of Waugh's satire, including Constantine himself, are judged.[68]

The other artistic flaw in *Helena* is Waugh's tendency to subordinate the story he is telling to the theme, which, ideally, should emerge from the story. This flaw is reflected in Waugh's concentration on the historical milieu of the story and the state of Christianity in Helena's time, which makes some passages of *Helena* read more like a historical essay than a novel. Had Waugh decided to make *Helena* a historical essay like his *Edmund Campion*, the reader would have no difficulty accepting this approach to the material.

Waugh's choice of a historical setting for the novel seems dictated in part at least by his desire to show the immutability of Christianity (specifically of Catholicism) in the pagan world of the fourth century and its continuity with the faith of the twentieth century. In all his other novels, the theme emerges through careful plotting and characterization. In this one novel Waugh seems to have decided on his theme — how Divine Providence gave a fourth-century saint the special vocation of reaffirming the truth of Christianity — and then engineered his fiction to emphasize his theme. Consequently one is more justified in criticizing Waugh, as Carens does, for imbuing *Helena* with a somewhat apologetic strain than one is in finding a similar purpose to be operative in *Brideshead Revisited*. The fact that Waugh succumbed only once to the temptation to subordinate story to theme brings his achievement in his other novels into sharper relief.

Waugh felt that the pagan elements in the world of his own time, which he had portrayed in *The Loved One*, had much in common with those in the Roman empire of St. Helena's time. Barbarism, he felt, was always with us and must always be combated. "Barbarism is never fully defeated," he wrote on the eve of World War II; "given propitious circumstances, men and women who seem quite orderly will commit every conceivable atrocity." We are all "potential recruits for anarchy."[69]

Love among the Ruins (1953)

Waugh now felt it time to depict the probable future of mankind in an increasingly barbarous world. He conceived the idea of writing "a romance of the near future" in 1951 during the Festival of Britain, which had been decreed, as he later put it in the last chapter of the *Sword of Honor* trilogy, "to celebrate the opening of a happier decade" than the one just past. "Monstrous constructions" such as the Dome of Discovery appeared on the south bank of the Thames, he continued, "but there was little popular exuberance among the straitened people" of Britain, "and dollar-bearing tourists curtailed their visits and sped to the countries of the Continent where, however precarious their condition, they ordered things better."

Waugh therefore published *Love among the Ruins* in 1953, the coronation year of Elizabeth II, as what his daughter Teresa calls "his ironic but comic comment on what he saw as the unjustified optimism of the time" Or, as Robert Murray Davis puts it, "*Love among the Ruins* is Waugh's non–love letter to Welfare State England, bleak and unlovely under the postwar austerity program instituted by Atlee's Labor government."[70]

In this novella religion is shown to have disappeared from man's life, replaced by the cult of the State. "State be with you" is the greeting heard as "Santa-Claus-Tide" draws near. Waugh had pointedly noted in the preface of *Vile Bodies* that "Christmas is observed by the Western Church on December 25th" for the benefit of future readers who might not be familiar with its celebration; in *Love among the Ruins* Santa Claus Day has indeed replaced Christmas Day.

The observance of the Day is marked by the annual performance on television of "an old obscure folk play" which has been "revived and revised as a matter of historical interest." It is a "strange spectacle of an ox and an ass, an old man with a lantern, and a young mother" which shows, among other things, how much maternity services have improved since the time in which the play is set. In one scene food production workers appear to have declared a sudden strike, left their sheep, and run off "at the bidding of some kind of shop-steward in fantastic dress." At this point a chorus breaks into an old, forgotten ditty: "Oh tidings of comfort and joy, comfort and joy." Thus the Nativity story has become mere fodder for state propaganda.

Despite imposing edifices such as the Dome of Security (Waugh's parody of the Festival of Britain's Dome of Discovery), which ostensibly testify to man's material progress, man himself has degenerated into a depersonalized servant of the State. Miles Plastic, as his last name implies, is the machine-tooled product of this new society:

> The State had made him. No clean-living, God-fearing, Victorian gentleman, he; no complete man of the Renaissance; no gentle knight nor dutiful pagan nor, even, noble savage. All the succession of past worthies had gone its way, content to play a prelude to Miles. He was the Modern Man. His history, as it appeared in multiple in the filing cabinets of numberless State departments, was typical of a thousand others.

"This little pile of papers is You," Miles is told by a public official; among the stack there is even a certificate attesting to the fact that Miles has a human personality, something that might not otherwise be apparent. Miles represents the final flowering of the superficially civilized modern man Waugh had drawn in Julia's husband Rex Mottram in *Brideshead Revisited.* Julia had thought at first that Rex was "a sort of primitive savage, but he was something absolutely modern and up-to-date that only this ghastly age could produce. A tiny bit of a man pretending he was the whole." One is also reminded of Sir Francis Hinsley in *The Loved One,* who found himself, after years of subservience to a film studio, to be a half-human whom the studio had to keep going with a pump in order that he might still be capable of a few crude reactions.

In Miles Plastic, Waugh is portraying in satiric terms the final fulfillment of the warning he had given as far back as 1930 and reiterated in the characters of Rex Mottram and Sir Francis Hinsley. In 1930 he had written:

> It is no longer possible . . . to accept the benefits of civilization and at the same time deny the supernatural basis upon which it rests. As the issues become clearer, the polite skeptic and with him that purely fictitious figure, the happy hedonist, will disappear.[71]

One character alone in the story resists the process of dehumanization imposed by the State. He is a convict who has been sent to prison for rehabilitation several times. He tells Miles that the first time he was sentenced, the judge warned him he was living a life that would lead to "degradation in this world and everlasting damnation in the next." The last time he was sentenced, he complains, he was merely termed "maladjusted" and an "antisocial phenomenon." Man in other words is no longer morally responsible for his own acts in the eyes of the State. Man in other words is no longer man.

Moreover, man is no longer capable of true love, though Miles is attracted to a ballet dancer named Clara, whose chief physical characteristic is a golden beard — the curious result of an unsuccessful sterilization operation. The beautiful hair of the girl in Browning's poem "Love among the Ruins" thus becomes in Waugh's tale the grotesque yellow beard of a female. Clara becomes pregnant by Miles and is directed by the authorities to undergo an operation in which a state doctor aborts the unborn child. The doctor also replaces Clara's beard with a skin graft of "a wonderful new substance, a sort of synthetic rubber." Miles is upset by the loss of the child and is revolted by Clara's tight, slippery, salmon-pink mask, which impresses him as "something quite inhuman." Miles comes to see in Clara a reflection of the synthetic being which he too has become and now realizes how well his last name is beginning to suit him. In protest he burns down the rehabilitation center in which Clara lies recovering and leaves his lost love among the ruins.

The State decrees that Miles is to marry a Miss Flower; but during the civil ceremony Miles's fingers fidget with the cigarette lighter in his pocket. Its tiny, gemlike flame will be the unobtrusive instrument by which he will continue his activities as an arsonist in order to defy the State and to reassert his humanity, by exercising his power to make decisions. The godless society which Waugh imagines in *Love among the Ruins* is the logical result of the paganizing tendencies in man which he had pointed out in *The Loved One* and in *Helena*. Miles's impersonal, machine-like civilization, which has abandoned all spiritual values, is in Waugh's view already in ruins. Miles needs only to finish the job.

Laura Waugh remembers that her husband noticed in retrospect that his later fiction, from *Brideshead Revisited* onward, contained some purple patches and that "he was particularly ashamed of the ones in *Love among the Ruins.*" Auberon Waugh adds, "After he had written that novelette my father was dissatisfied with it because it was too self-consciously obvious in depicting its theme, though he still very much endorsed that theme."

Love among the Ruins, like *The Loved One*, has some witty and meaningful passages; but, like *Helena*, it is uneven and somewhat contrived. The characters are *papier-mâché*, not sufficiently real to engage the reader fully; the novella therefore is not in a class with *The Loved One*. However, I very much agree with James Carens that *Love among the Ruins* is most valuable not as a prophecy about life in a future godless society but as a revelation that the ruins which Waugh describes already surround us: Waugh "has carried to certain extremes of exaggeration tendencies which already undeniably exist."[72]

Since *Helena* and *Love among the Ruins* are Waugh's only attempts to write fiction not set in his own era, the critic Paul Doyle has formulated the axiom that "Waugh's hand becomes unsteady and less convincing if he cannot work within the realism of his own period and from the authenticity of personal experience."[73]

Each of the three works considered in this chapter fulfills in its own way Waugh's intent of dealing with man in his relation to God, a goal stated at the time he published *Brideshead*. *Helena* presents Waugh's theme positively and directly by showing a saint who was deeply conscious of her duty to God in living out her life, a thought which permeated Waugh's own thinking. The two satires present Waugh's theme negatively and by indirection, by showing man's gradual estrangement from God and the absurdities to which it leads. *The Loved One* is the better satire of the two and remains the best work Waugh composed in the period between *Brideshead* and the *Sword of Honor* trilogy.

The "minor trilogy" just considered contains one primarily serious novel, *Helena*, and two satires. In his war trilogy, Waugh was to take the raw material of his army experiences and weave them into an integrated work of art, blending satirical with serious elements throughout. In so doing he would not only present his personal vision in a moving fashion; he would produce a major work of fiction that would equal — and perhaps surpass — his achievement in *Brideshead Revisited*. And now to war with Waugh.

6

The Unhappy Warrior: The *Sword of Honor* Trilogy

"In the preposterous years of the Second World War, I collected enough experience to last several lifetimes of novel writing," Waugh wrote in *Life* after the war (8 April 1946). Indeed, Waugh is one of the few major novelists of his generation to be able to draw on firsthand experience of World War II. There are many parallels between the army career of Waugh's hero, Guy Crouchback, and that of Waugh himself.

Waugh was commissioned in the Royal Marines in 1939 and took part in the Dakar campaign against the Vichy French in the summer of 1940. In 1941 he went to the Middle East to serve with the Commandos and participated in their raid on Bardia. He was later transferred to the Horse Guards and was in the battle of Crete as a member of the commander's personal staff. In 1943, as an officer in the Airborne Corps, Waugh underwent parachute training and twisted his knee in a practice jump. He returned to active duty in June 1944, when he and Randolph Churchill joined Brigadier General Maclean's Special Air Service in its mission to Yugoslavia to help Marshal Tito's guerrillas hold back the Nazi invasion. The plane taking them to Yugoslavia crashed, and only Waugh, Churchill, and one other occupant survived. After convalescing in Algiers, they went on to Yugoslavia to join their comrades in fulfilling their mission.

With this military experience behind him, Waugh told the *New York Times,* "I do want to write a novel about the war; it would be a study of chivalry" (13 March 1949). Waugh's intention, as he outlined it in his preface to the 1965 one-volume edition of his war trilogy, was "to give a description of the Second World War as it was seen and experienced by a single, uncharacteristic Englishman, and to show its effect on him." In December 1951, Waugh wrote to Thomas Merton, "I am just coming to the end of the first volume of what I hope will be a series of works covering the whole of the last war. It has some good bits of pure farce but much that is dull and trite."[74] Despite this modest disclaimer of the merits of *Men at Arms* (1952), Waugh continued to work on his opus and published *Officers and Gentlemen* in 1955.

"Originally I had intended the second volume, *Officers and Gentlemen,* to be two volumes," Waugh explained afterward. "Then I decided to lump them together and finish it off."[75] Waugh's devoted readers were upset when he announced that his war novels, originally planned as a trilogy, would end with *Officers and Gentlemen.* English critic Maryvonne Butcher wrote that apparently Waugh had tired of his project, "and like a bored child roughly bundled a hurried conclusion on the end of his second volume." One felt at the time, she said, slightly cheated at the summary way in which Waugh had dealt with some of his characters. "Indeed, characters and readers alike looked up like Milton's hungry sheep, and were not fed."[76]

Then, almost a decade after the first volume of the trilogy had appeared, Waugh decided to complete the trilogy with *Unconditional Surrender* (1961), titled *The End of the Battle* in the United States. "The third volume really arose from the fact that Ludovic," an eccentric and intriguing character, "needed explaining," Waugh noted. "As it turned out, each volume had a common form because there was an irrelevant ludicrous figure in each": Apthorpe in *Men at Arms,* Trimmer in *Officers and Gentlemen,* and Ludovic in *Unconditional Surrender.*

Although Waugh had found that the trilogy "changed a lot in writing," he also pointed out that most of the elements were "there from the beginning," for example, the controlling imagery of the sword of Sir Roger the Crusader.[77] In fact, as Waugh confesses in the preface to the one-volume edition, "the less than candid assurance" that each of the three novels as it appeared "was to be regarded as a separate, independent work" was dictated by commercial considerations. From the outset, he admits, he designed the trilogy to be read as a single story.

Waugh felt, however, that because the three books had been written at intervals during a decade, repetitions and discrepancies had crept into the work. These he excised, along with passages which, "on rereading, appeared tedious," when he revised the trilogy for publication in one volume under the overall title *Sword of Honor* in 1965. The minor revisions Waugh made to ensure that the three separately published books would blend smoothly into a single story are readily understandable. Several incidental characters have been deprived of names in order to shorten the otherwise enormous list of names the reader is to keep in mind. These characters are now referred to by such general names as "the sergeant" or "the second-in-command." For the same reason, a few minor characters have disappeared altogether — for instance Hemp, Guy Crouchback's fellow Catholic officer in *Men at Arms*, who was not "over scrupulous in his religious duties from which (he claimed to have read somewhere), all servicemen were categorically dispensed."

Aside from these few exceptions, I find that most if not all of the other excisions which Waugh made in the text of the novels on grounds of repetition or tedium are simply unjustified. If a reader does not get caught up in the sweep of Waugh's panoramic picture of World War II, the omission of a paragraph here and a page there will not win him. In addition, most of the passages cut are delightful vignettes which "only an author prodigal of wit could have sacrificed," as critic Andrew Rutherford puts it.[78]

For example, gone is the bingo game which Brigadier Ritchie-Hook, Guy's eccentric commanding officer, organizes during

Guy's officers' training course to show that his battle strategy of out-foxing the enemy — which he calls "biffing" — applies even at the bingo table. Gone is the American historical film in which Bonnie Prince Charlie speaks in "rich Milwaukee accents." And gone is the naughty song which the befuddled Air Marshall Beech recites at a party, to everyone's embarrassment but his own:

> Would you like to sin
> With Eleanor Glyn
> On a tiger skin?
> Or would you prefer
> With her to err
> On some other fur?

I will note more examples of deleted passages as I treat the trilogy. I could not agree more with the judgment of the *London Times Literary Supplement:* "If the real idea . . . was to keep the book to 800 pages and fifty shillings [about $6.50] it was a short-sighted piece of economy."[79] The only valid artistic reason which Waugh could have had for cutting these episodes would have been to insure that his serious religious theme would not be lost in an over-long story. But in fact, the theme emerges with equal clarity in the three separate volumes of the trilogy and in the *Sword of Honor* recension.

Waugh raises another important point in his preface to *Sword of Honor.* He says that, without realizing it, he had written in his trilogy "an obituary of the Roman Catholic Church in England as it existed for many centuries":

All the rites and most of the opinions here described are already obsolete. . . . It never occurred to me, writing *Sword of Honor,* that the Church was susceptible to change. I was wrong and I have seen a superficial revolution in what then seemed permanent. Despite the faith of many of the characters, *Sword of Honor* was not specifically a religious book. Recent developments have made it, in fact, a document of Catholic usage of my youth.

This remark was an afterthought, says Auberon Waugh, "attributable to the fact that he was so taken up at the time that he wrote the preface with the idea of renewal within the Church. By then the changes, mostly liturgical, which he had feared would come about in the Church because of the Second Vatican Council in the early 1960's had in fact become a reality." Even Waugh's friend and fellow convert, Msgr. Ronald Knox (who died in 1957 before Vatican II had convened), had "lived to see the Roman Church abandon many of the features which he had emulated as an Anglican," as Waugh wrote in his life of Knox. "Some of his later sermons . . . are rebukes addressed to himself for his sentimental regret at the changing face of the Church."[80]

Waugh himself, however, became increasingly dismayed with the introduction of doctrinal and liturgical reform into a church he had so admired when he joined it as a convert thirty years before. Theologian Hubert Van Zeller has tried to explain Waugh's feelings toward the renewal *(aggiornamento)* in the Catholic church in this way:

> The *aggiornamento* spelled for him a repudiation of the Church's inflexibility. The new freedoms meant to him a negation rather than an affirmation. He had come to know the Church which was built upon a rock, and now he saw the rock moving out to sea. It was especially in the matter of the liturgy, as English-speaking Catholics soon learned, that he felt himself to be adrift. He had expected permanence in the use of Latin for the Mass, in an established ceremonial, and suddenly he was presented with what threatened to be a free-for-all.[81]

As Waugh wrote in the *National Review*, the reformers, as far as he was concerned, were trying to give the Church "the character of our own deplorable epoch" (4 December 1962). And in that statement lies the key to Waugh's attitude toward renewal in the Catholic church. Waugh looked upon such reforms as symptomatic of a phenomenon he had already made the basis of satire in *The Loved One, Love among the Ruins,* and other works of fiction: that is, the loss of respect in his era for all the traditional values he cherished. When Waugh's remark that *Sword of Honor* is an obituary for the Roman Catholic church of his youth is taken in this larger context, one can see the far-reaching implications it had for him.

In addition, the casual references in the trilogy to the religious services and feast days of the Catholic church serve as a gentle reminder of the supernatural order that, Waugh feels, persists amid the chaos of war. As James Carens suggests, Waugh's allusions to Catholic ritual in the trilogy "are in no sense obtrusive; they form an inevitable part of the pattern of Guy Crouchback's existence. Guy's elderly father, who is often associated with these observances and rituals, embodies Waugh's social and religious ideals."[82]

Waugh was disillusioned about his life in the army as well as his life in the Church, as is apparent in the trilogy. In his own words, the trilogy can be taken as "a kind of uncelebration, a history of Guy Crouchback's disillusion with the army. Guy has old fashioned ideas of honor and illusions of chivalry; we see these being used up and destroyed by his encounters with the realities of army life."[83] Guy's progressive disillusionment with the army provides the structural framework for each of the three books. His disenchantment with the army is paralleled by Ronald Knox's reaction to the loss of so many of his friends in World War I, as recounted by Waugh in his life of Knox: "Their sacrifice seemed, more plainly each year, to have been quite in vain in realizing 'the England of their dreams.'"[84]

The critic Malcolm Bradbury sums up the trilogy's mood of disenchantment this way:

> All three books begin in light spirit with a series of events in training, set in England, with Guy's mood a hopeful one, and all conclude with events in action abroad, where Guy witnesses and is involved in a betrayal, as a result of which he suffers in reputation, hope and faith.[85]

The thematic unity of the trilogy arises from the fact that in his progress through the trilogy, Guy is searching for a workable system of values to replace his earlier illusions, one which will help him cope with the disappointments and frustrations he experiences. In taking up *Sword of Honor*, I shall treat each of the three volumes in turn, within the context of the overall structural and thematic unity they gain by being part of the single story Waugh designed them to be from the start.

Men at Arms (1952)

Men at Arms begins in August 1939 with Guy's decision, at the age of thirty-five, to enlist in the service of his country at the outbreak of World War II. Eight years before, Guy had been divorced by his promiscuous wife, ironically named Virginia. Because Virginia has had two additional husbands since she divorced Guy, not to mention an assortment of lovers, she has much in common with Brenda, Tony Last's wife in *A Handful of Dust*.

Ever since the divorce, Guy has lived in seclusion in the Crouchback villa in Santa Dulcina, Italy. War has threatened for some time, but for Guy the issues do not become clear until the Russian-German alliance is signed by Von Ribbentrop and Molotov. Together the Nazi and Communist credos epitomize for Guy all the forces of the modern age which are obliterating those traditional values of western Christian civilization he holds dear:

> Eight years of shame and loneliness were ended. For eight years Guy, already set apart from his fellows by his own deep wound, that unstaunched, internal draining away of life and love, had been deprived of the loyalties which should have sustained him. . . . But now, splendidly, everything had become clear. The enemy at last was plain in view, huge and hateful, all disguises cast off. It was the Modern Age in arms. Whatever the outcome there was a place for him in the battle.

Before setting out for England to join the army, Guy visits once more the tomb of Sir Roger of Waybroke, an English knight buried in the parish church. Sir Roger had sailed from Genoa eight hundred years before for the Second Crusade, but was shipwrecked on the coast near Santa Dulcina:

> There he enlisted under the local Count, who promised to take him to the Holy Land but led him first against a neighbor, on the walls of whose castle he fell at the moment of victory. The Count

gave him honorable burial and there he had lain through the centuries, . . . a man with a great journey still all before him and a great vow unfulfilled; but the people of Santa Dulcina . . . brought him their troubles and touched his sword for luck, so that its edge was always bright.

All his life, Guy had felt a close kinship with *il Santo Inglese* ("the English saint"). Now, on his last day, he visits the tomb and runs his finger along the knight's sword, as the local fishermen always do before setting out. "Sir Roger, pray for me," he murmurs, "and for our endangered kingdom."

Guy's piety is rooted in that of his family — a venerable English Catholic family whose ancestral home at Broome has never lacked a priest for its chapel, even during times when some of Guy's forebears, such as Blessed Gervase Crouchback, were sent to the scaffold: Guy's father, Gervase Crouchback, has derived a serene faith from his ancestors which enables him to accept misfortune as part of the plan of Divine Providence:

He was an innocent, affable old man who had somehow preserved his good humor — much more than that, a mysterious and tranquil joy — throughout a life which to all outward observation had been overloaded with misfortune. He had like many another been born in full sunlight and lived to see night fall. He had an ancient name which was now little regarded and threatened with extinction.

When Mr. Crouchback could no longer maintain Broome and leased it to a Catholic girls' boarding school (as Waugh himself did his home in Gloucestershire during the war), he did not consider his ancestral home lost to the family. In his actual leave-taking of Broome, Mr. Crouchback had not even complained, Waugh writes in a charming passage which does not appear in *Sword of Honor.* I reproduce it here almost in full as an example of one of the gems lost in Waugh's revision of *Sword of Honor:*

He attended every day of the sale seated in the marquee on the auctioneer's platform, munching pheasant sandwiches, drinking port from a flask and watching the bidding with tireless interest, all unlike the ruined squire of Victorian iconography. . . . "Awful shabby the carpets look when you get them out. . . . What on earth can Mrs. Chadwick want with a stuffed bear?"

Mr. Crouchback took solace in the fact that, though the Crouchbacks no longer inhabited Broome, "the sanctuary lamp still burned at Broome as of old." Unlike the sanctuary lamp in the chapel of the wayward Marchmain family in *Brideshead Revisited*, which had been put out when the family chapel was closed for a time, the flame of faith has always burned brightly at Broome. That faith is epitomized in Mr. Crouchback himself, whom Waugh intended to keep audible in the trilogy "a steady undertone of the decencies and true purpose of life behind the chaos of events and fantastic characters. Also to show him as a typical victim (parallel to the trainloads going to concentration camps) in the war against the Modern Age."[86] In addition, Waugh's official biographer, Christopher Sykes (to whom the second volume of the trilogy is dedicated), has written to me that he believes Waugh's own religious attitudes to be "most precisely expressed in the character of Crouchback Senior in his war trilogy."

In contrast to his father, who draws great consolation from his simple faith, Guy sees himself as "destitute, possessed of nothing save a few dry grains of faith." Guy is afflicted with what St. Thomas Aquinas called *accidia*, a Latin term which can be translated as "spiritual sloth." In his essay on "Sloth" in a collection called *The Seven Capital Sins*, Waugh uses the term as Aquinas did, as *tristitia de bono spirituali*, "sadness in the face of spiritual good":

Man is made for joy in the love of God, a love which he expresses in service. If he deliberately turns away from that joy, he is denying the purpose of his existence. The malice of Sloth lies not merely in the neglect of duty (though that can be a symptom of it) but in the refusal of joy. It is allied to despair. . . . Sloth is the condition in which a man is fully aware of the proper means of his salvation and refuses to take them because the whole apparatus of salvation fills him with tedium and disgust.[87]

Guy's is an arrested case of this sloth; he loyally practices his faith, but it does not bring him joy as it does to his father. Guy has even joined the army in an effort to shake off this spiritual malady by reestablishing his interest in other people and somehow being of service to his fellow man. Because his soul languishes in a wasteland that even he cannot understand, Guy's practice of his religion is perfunctory. "Even in his religion he felt no brotherhood. Often he wished that he lived in penal times when Broome had been a solitary outpost of the faith, surrounded by aliens. Sometimes he imagined himself serving the last mass for the last Pope in a catacomb at the end of the world."

As Msgr. Ronald Knox points out, "Guy Crouchback remains isolated, and to a certain extent handicapped, by belonging to a religion and a culture older and more orderly than anything which lies within the ken of his oddly assorted mess-mates; yet the army, for him, is an integrating factor in his life (as marriage is for other men, but cannot be for him)."[88] In an effort to convince himself that his religion should give some meaning to his arid life, Guy earnestly asks an army chaplain (in words reminiscent of Charles Ryder's in *Brideshead Revisited*), "Do you agree . . . that the Supernatural Order is not something added to the Natural Order, like music or painting, to make everyday life more tolerable? It *is* everyday life. The supernatural is real; what we call 'real' is a mere shadow, a passing fancy."

Perhaps Mr. Crouchback is trying to communicate to Guy a share in the consolation his faith gives him — a consolation he finds totally absent in Guy — when he presents Guy with the medal of Our Lady of Lourdes which Guy's older brother (Gervase, Jr.) had worn until his death in World War I. Guy uses the medal as a reminder not only of the spiritual support prayer can give but also of the spirit of his energetic and more optimistic older brother, Gervase.

Since his divorce Guy has fallen into "a habit of dry and negative chastity which even the priests felt to be unedifying. On the lowest, as on the highest plane, there was no sympathy between him and his fellow men." Guy is plagued by the fact that he has no heir to carry on the Crouchback name, since as a Roman Catholic he cannot remarry. His sister Angela's husband, Arthur Box-Bender, who is not a Catholic, cannot understand why Guy does not remarry anyway, a point of view that is incomprehensible to Guy's father:

> When Virginia left Guy childless, it did not occur to Mr. Crouchback, as it had never ceased occurring to Box-Bender, that the continuance of his line was worth a tiff with the Church; that Guy should marry by civil law and beget an heir and settle things up later with the ecclesiastical authorities as other people seemed somehow to do. Family pride could not be served in dishonor.

By chance Guy makes the acquaintance of Mr. Ambrose Goodall, who is well versed in the history of Catholicism in England. Mr. Goodall tells Guy of a situation similar to Guy's own in a "historic Catholic family" some fifty years back. The last heir of the family was divorced by his wife, but later they met abroad and had a brief affair resulting in a child who grew up to perpetuate the family name. Mr. Goodall is careful to point out that the man committed no sin in going to bed with his former wife because in the eyes of the Church they were still married. Guy is intrigued by the story, especially because Mr. Goodall looks upon the whole episode as a manifestation of Divine Providence. "Mr. Goodall," asks Guy, "do you seriously believe that God's Providence concerns itself with the perpetuation of the English Catholic aristocracy?" Mr. Goodall is unruffled in his response: "But of course. And with sparrows, too, we are taught."

Guy's conversation with Mr. Goodall prompts him to arrange to spend an evening with Virginia in London while he is on leave, appropriately on St. Valentine's Day. Guy encourages Virginia to become amorous. They are on the point of making love when Virginia realizes that Guy is only interested in her because she is "the only woman in the world your priests would let you go to bed with." As Guy returns to camp he realizes there is no hope for reconciliation with Virginia in the foreseeable future.

Guy is a member of the Royal Corps of Halberdiers, and because of his age and the shortage of officers at the outbreak of the war, he is already enrolled in an officers' training program ·Guy's idealism about the cause for which he has enlisted grows during the early period of his training. His romantic view of military service is rooted not only in his devotion to Sir Roger but also in his memories of the Captain Truslove stories he had read as a boy — adventures more real to Guy in his youth "than the world of mud and wire and gas where Gervase fell." Waugh must have thought that the Truslove passages overemphasized Guy's romanticism, since all of them have been cut in *Sword of Honor*.

Slowly, almost imperceptibly, Guy is becoming aware that the war which he is engaged in is not the pilgrimage he had once thought, but a conflict in which "courage and a just cause were quite irrelevant to the issue." Nor is he the crusader that he had once fancied himself. At the conclusion of his officers' training program, "he just scraped through without honors. Guy felt no resentment. . . . He merely felt a deep sinking of spirit; Sir Roger, maybe, had felt thus when he drew his dedicated sword in a local brawl."

Guy's love affair with the army, like Charles Ryder's, results (like both of their marriages) in disenchantment and alienation of affection. In Guy's case, Guy is at least partially to blame if the army has failed to live up to his expectations; his romantic illusions that army life should correspond to Sir Roger's crusade (and to the exploits of Captain Truslove) could never have been realized.

Apthorpe, Guy's good-natured but immature fellow junior officer — the only one as old as Guy — helps to melt the chilly atmosphere with which Guy surrounds himself. In his friendship with Apthorpe, Guy (like Charles Ryder in his friendship with Sebastian) experiences something he never had, "a happy adolescence." Appropriately, the officers' training program in which Guy meets Apthorpe is carried on in a former prep school for boys. Apthorpe is the occasion of Guy's first genuine attempts to help others as he begins to realize that the love of God must be expressed in charity — something he does not understand fully until late in the trilogy. Guy's willingness to help Apthorpe hide the latter's "Thunderbox" (a portable latrine for use in the field) so that Apthorpe can preserve it for his own exclusive use is a comic example of Guy's growing interest in others.

Guy sails with the Dakar expedition, in the course of which Ritchie-Hook takes it upon himself to ask Guy to lead an unauthorized reconnaissance mission onto the African coast. Guy agrees because the whole operation makes him feel temporarily identified once more with Captain Truslove.

In *Life* magazine, Waugh described firsthand the real raid on an enemy coastline which the incident in *Men at Arms* parodies. In Waugh's real-life account:

> The boats hit the beach in line, emptied and then reversed their engines. The boats and men were out of sight in opposite directions within a few seconds. . . . There was silence for about half an hour. Various parties were setting their demolition charges. Suddenly from all sides detonations began. . . . The work finished, we returned to our beaches. The way down was lit by burning stores. The boats now came back to the beaches. . . . The timetable had worked out to the minute with nothing to spare. (17 November 1941)

But the fictional raid turns into a fiasco when Ritchie-Hook goes along incognito in order to bring back as a souvenir the head of an African sentry. The last shred of Guy's romantic view of the army is destroyed when he is blamed for the whole affair and recalled to England. For the rest of his life, he is told, when his name comes up someone will be bound to say, "Isn't he the chap who blotted his copybook at Dakar in '40?"

Guy's spiritual sloth deepens when he comes under further official disapproval. As a friendly gesture toward Apthorpe, Guy gives his ailing hospitalized friend a bottle of whiskey. Apthorpe characteristically drinks too much too soon and dies. Guy returns to England with two black marks against him and with a sense of disaster.

Apthorpe had to die, for he symbolizes the high spirits and optimism with which Guy entered the service and which have been drained from him in the course of Men at Arms. Waugh eliminated Apthorpe at the novel's end because he realized that Apthorpe belonged to Guy's belated adolescence and would not fit into the increasingly serious atmosphere of the latter volumes.

Msgr. Ronald Knox notes in his review of Men at Arms that as the novel nears its end, Waugh's treatment of Apthorpe becomes more and more realistic, even though Apthorpe remains essentially a comic creation. At the end Apthorpe definitely belongs to the real world, in which the most ridiculous of us must be dignified, sooner or later, by the touch of death: "Apthorpe's last moments are invested with an almost intolerable pathos" by his admission that his wealthy aristocratic aunt "was only an invention. He could so easily have carried the secret to his grave, and we should have been none the wiser. Yet somehow the unreality of his pedigree makes Apthorpe more real to us than ever."[89]

Officers and Gentlemen (1955)

"*Men at Arms* ended with the death of Apthorpe," Waugh wrote in his introduction to the second volume of the trilogy. "*Officers and Gentlemen* begins with the placation of his spirit. A ritual preparation for the descent into the nether world of Crete."

Apthorpe's dying request of Guy was that Guy should deliver all his belongings to another friend, Chatty Corner. This task occupies Guy at the beginning of *Officers and Gentlemen:*

So Guy set out on another stage of his pilgrimage, which had begun at the tomb of Sir Roger. Now, as then, an act of *pietas* was required of him, a spirit to be placated. Apthorpe's gear must be retrieved and delivered before Guy was free to follow his fortunes in the King's service.

The second novel of the trilogy is made up of two sections which together contain the material Waugh had originally intended to comprise both the second and third volumes. Possibly he realized that the material now contained in the first section of *Officers and Gentlemen* was too skimpy to form a volume by itself. Waugh decided to "lump them together and finish it off." Accordingly he provided what he later considered "a bad transitional passage," set on board a troopship en route to the Middle East. This "Interlude," as Waugh titled it, was to link the two sections into one novel.[90]

Book I of *Officers and Gentlemen*, based on the training program Waugh underwent in Scotland, deals with Guy's training as a commando on the Isle of Mugg in Scotland. Guy has returned to England and receives his orders at Marchmain House, former London home of the Marchmain family in *Brideshead Revisited*, which has been given over to the use of Hazardous Offensive Operations Headquarters. Before reporting to the training camp, Guy manages to cut through a great deal of red tape and deliver Apthorpe's gear to Chatty Corner. For Guy it is a gesture of loyalty to his deceased friend. As Chatty signs a receipt for Apthorpe's kit, Guy senses that this is a "holy moment," for the spirit of Apthorpe is now placated.

Now Guy is ready to undergo his training as a commando in preparation for the expedition to Crete, described in Book II; the objective is to save the island of Crete from the German advance. On Mugg, Guy again meets Trimmer, a former Halberdier who had been dropped from the officers' training program in which Guy participated. Trimmer has changed his name to McTavish and gotten a fresh start. Lord Ian Kilbannock, an army press officer, later chooses Trimmer to lead a minor raid on an unimportant island in order to provide copy for his press dispatches. Trimmer's expedition, appropriately called

"Operation Popgun," is even more ludicrous than Guy's raid in Africa had been. By mistake the party lands on the coast of occupied France. Trimmer is terrified the whole time, but one of his men takes this opportunity to blow up a railroad track.

The result of Trimmer's foray into enemy territory strikingly contrasts with the outcome of Guy's patrol in Africa. Whereas Guy "blotted his copybook," Trimmer becomes a national hero through the machinations of Lord Kilbannock, who uses the incident as a publicity ploy to raise morale on the home front. Moreover, Kilbannock discovers that Virginia had a short-lived affair with Trimmer, once her hairdresser. He persuades the reluctant Virginia to resume the relationship in order to bolster Trimmer's own morale for his public appearances as Trimmer tours England for the edification of the populace. Sexual immorality, Waugh suggests, is part of the general erosion of moral values initiated by the war. All kinds of questionable behavior can now be justified in the name of "expediency." The critic Andrew Rutherford gets at the irony Waugh intended in this passage when he notes that Ian Kilbannock's cynicism, "amusing at first, is revealed as hateful and corrupting." Kilbannock's build-up of Trimmer as a hero is symptomatic of "the replacement of truth and honor by propaganda as the Modern Age girds on its arms."[91] Yet Ian continues to be respected as a peer and a member of Bellamy's, an exclusive gentlemen's club in London.

The disintegration of moral fiber is further evidenced in Ivor Claire, an officer with whom Guy has become friendly since the death of Apthorpe. Guy is attracted to Claire because Guy believes that both he and Claire see life *sub specie aeternitatis* ("in the light of eternity") and with "a melancholy sense of humor." But Guy fails to see that Ivor is an effeminate — if not homosexual — aesthete like Ambrose Silk in *Put Out More Flags* (Ivor's last name bears the French feminine gender ending). When Guy meet Ivor, Ivor is reclining on a sofa wiping the face of Freda, his Pekinese, with a silk handkerchief. Nonetheless Guy, with a confidence in

Ivor he lives to regret, prefers to think of Ivor "putting his horse faultlessly over the jumps, concentrated as a nun in prayer. Ivor Claire, Guy thought, was the fine flower of them all. He was the quintessential England, the man Hitler had not taken into account." In short, Guy respects Ivor as an officer and a gentleman, a combination that Guy realizes is becoming increasingly rare.

The combination is even rarer in *Sword of Honor* than in *Officers and Gentlemen*, for Waugh has completely deleted from the revised version of the trilogy any reference to General Miltiades, an elderly Greek officer whom Guy meets on Crete when the battle is going against the British:

> The old man was rather small, very upright, very brown, very wrinkled, with superb white moustaches and three lines of decorations. . . . He was past seventy. In youth he had fought the Turks and been often wounded. In middle life the politicians had often sent him into exile. In old age he was homeless again, finally, it might seem, still following his kind. . . . Mugs were filled. The general had some English. He proposed a toast; with no shade of irony in his steady, pouchy eyes; the single word: "Victory."

Since General Miltiades does not appear in *Sword of Honor*, we also lose the significant remark which Ludovic, one of Ivor Claire's subordinates, records in his diary about the General: "Captain Crouchback . . . is pleased because General Miltiades is a gentleman. He would like to believe that the war is being fought by such people. But all gentlemen are now very old." Men like the General and Guy's father are members of a vanishing race, the demise of which is leaving room for opportunists like Trimmer and like Ludovic, who resembles "a dishonest valet."

Guy's spiritual sloth is growing in direct proportion to his degree of disenchantment with the army, to which Ludovic referred above. He even visits a nearby town to make his Easter confession instead of going to the camp chaplain: "Already, without deliberation, he had begun to dissociate himself from the army in matters of real concern." Later it develops that the priest who heard his confession is an enemy spy. This incident was based on Waugh's own "genuine experience," as he mentions in a letter to Dame Edith Sitwell, commenting that "all priests are not as clean and kind as Father D'Arcy and Father Caraman," two Jesuits of their mutual acquaintance."[92] As it appears in *Officers and Gentlemen,* the episode represents yet another unsettling experience for Guy's ebbing morale. And there are more to come.

The attempt to rid Crete of the Nazis ends in ignominious defeat. As the Germans continue their advance, the British army falls into a complete state of rout. No one seems to be in charge. Chaos reigns. Ludovic and one of Guy's superior officers, Major "Fido" Hound, desert separately but meet in a cave on the south coast. "Nothing more is ever heard of Hound," says Waugh in his synopsis of the first two volumes of the trilogy, which he appended to the third volume when it appeared. "It is to be supposed that Ludovic perpetrated or contrived at his murder" — presumably to get rid of the only witness to his desertion.

Waugh goes on to summarize neatly the events of the day:

> On the morning of the surrender Guy meets Ludovic on the beach. They join a small party escaping by boat. They suffer acutely from privation and exposure. Ludovic alone remains capable. The delirious sapper officer who was originally in command disappears overboard during the night. It is to be supposed that Ludovic precipitated him. Finally they reach the African coast. Ludovic carries Guy ashore and, while he is half-conscious in hospital, is sent back to England to be decorated and commissioned. Ludovic believes that Guy knows the truth of the disappearance of "Fido" Hound.

Harriet Waugh remembers her father's recounting that the incompetence of the high command, coupled with the cowardice of certain officers, brought about the debacle of Crete: "When the surrender was announced most of the men threw down their arms, but my father didn't. He felt that surrender was dishonorable and even considered swimming out to sea in the hope that he would meet a boat that could take him aboard, instead of remaining on Crete and endorsing the surrender. In actual fact one of the officers secured a boat and picked up the men who had refused to surrender."

The cowardice of Major Hound, which Waugh used to symbolize the general disruption of morale and discipline among the British forces on Crete, was suggested by a fellow officer of Waugh's, whom I shall call here by the name Waugh gave him in the novel. In recalling in his diary the events that surrounded the British departure, Waugh says he was dispatched with orders for Lieutenant-Colonel Hound but could not find him. He finally located Hound in a tin-roofed shed, hunched up under a table "like a disconsolate ape," waiting out an air attack. When the planes retired, Hound emerged. "He still looked a soldierly figure when he was on his feet." Hound insisted that they march all night in order to avoid enemy gunfire. Nothing but daylight would stop him, and the moment that came "he popped into a drain under the road and sat there" (26 May 1941).

The cowardice of men like Hound and the overall disintegration of the British forces on Crete crush Guy's last illusions about the integrity with which the war effort is being conducted, just as it crushed Waugh's.

Guy lies for days in the hospital recalling his recent ordeal and refusing to speak to anyone: "Once he spoke he would reenter their world." When Guy finally does reestablish contact with those around him, he receives a jolt. He learns that Ivor Claire, officer and gentleman, though designated to remain behind with the rear guard which was to surrender Crete to the Germans, had deserted his troops and escaped with the others. Earlier Claire had said to Guy that honor is a changing thing; in the next war, he had predicted, "it will be quite honorable for officers to leave their men behind. . . . I reckon our trouble is that we're at the awkward stage."

The erosion of traditional values is such that by the end of the war and of the trilogy, Ivor Claire's "brief period of disgrace" has been all but forgotten. Even Guy later says of him, "Ivor doesn't believe in sacrifice. Who does nowadays?"

The ubiquitous Julia Stitch, who also appeared in *Scoop* (1938) and in *Put Out More Flags* (1942), turns up in Africa intent on saving her old friend Ivor from any further embarrassment. She succeeds because of her connections among the military. Guy too needs her help. During the chaos of Crete he had discovered the body of a British soldier:

> He lay as though at rest. The few corpses which Guy had seen in Crete had sprawled awkwardly. This soldier lay like an effigy on a tomb — like Sir Roger in his shadowy shrine at Santa Dulcina.... A precept came to Guy's mind from his military education: "The officer in command of a burial party is responsible for collecting the red identity discs and forwarding them to Records."

Guy kneels and removes from the body the red identity disc, which indicates that the dead man is a Roman Catholic. "May his soul and the souls of all the faithful departed, in the mercy of God, rest in peace," Guy prays. Then he stands, salutes, and moves on.

This episode had its origin in something that happened to Waugh during the last days on Crete. A peasant girl took him to a churchyard where she showed him the body of a British soldier on a stretcher, whom Waugh then arranged to have given a Catholic burial. How deeply moved Waugh was by the incident is clear from the tone in which he describes it in *Officers and Gentlemen*.

Guy entrusts the red identity disc to Julia in an envelope addressed to the proper authorities. But Julia, who is aware that Guy knows of Ivor's desertion, fears the envelope may contain evidence against Ivor. In *Sword of Honor* Waugh states explicitly what he only implies at the end of *Officers and Gentlemen*: that instead of delivering the envelope as she promised, she drops it into a wastebasket. Guy's act of service to a dead comrade, who seems to him more worthy of Sir Roger's memory than Guy himself does, is apparently circumvented by the irresponsible Julia. But Guy has done his duty nevertheless. He has not allowed his personal desolation to dissipate entirely his will to serve others — a fact that becomes increasingly important as the trilogy moves toward its conclusion.

The severest blow Guy has yet had to absorb comes on 22 June 1941, "a day of apocalypse for all the world for numberless generations," the day on which Nazi Germany invades Russia and it becomes clear that Russia will join the Allies. As far as Guy is concerned, his pilgrimage, which began at the tomb of Sir Roger, has come to an ignominious end. Two short years before, when the Allies were preparing to battle both Russia and Germany, it had seemed that a decade of shame was ending in light and reason:

> The Enemy was plain in view, huge and hateful, all disguise cast off; the Modern Age in arms. Now that hallucination was dissolved . . . and he was back after less than two years' pilgrimage in a Holy Land of illusion in the old ambiguous world, where priests were spies and gallant friends proved traitors and his country was led blundering into dishonor.

Guy's feelings about Russia were doubtless Waugh's as well. As early as 1930 Waugh had written: "The loss of faith in Christianity and the consequent lack of confidence in moral and social standards have become embodied in the ideal of a materialistic, mechanized state, already existent in Russia and rapidly spreading south and west."[93] In his diary entry for Easter Sunday 1945, Waugh notes a conversation at Campion Hall, the Jesuit College at Oxford, in which the participants were mostly despondent at the "collapse of Europe, the advance of Russia, heathenism." Waugh wryly concludes that he recommended a return to the catacombs of the early Christian era as the only refuge for any right thinking person.

Two of Waugh's companions in the army have recalled his feelings about Communism. Lord Birkenhead says that while he and Waugh were together in Yugoslavia, Waugh's "Catholic soul was filled with revulsion by the Communists who surrounded us, and were alleged to be our allies." Christopher Sykes adds, "When the war was over Evelyn was a bitter, disillusioned, angry man. He was horrified to think that we had defeated Nazi Germany only in alliance with Soviet Russia and with Hitler's equal in crime, Stalin. He was on bad terms with his times."[94] And so is

Guy Crouchback at this point. In Waugh's own words at the beginning of the trilogy's third volume, "As Guy, in the late autumn of 1941, rejoins his regiment he believes that the just cause of going to war has been forfeited in the Russian alliance. Personal honor alone remains."

Waugh's handling of the fall of Crete is an example of how deftly he has controlled his material in order to allow its thematic implications to emerge. For instance Trimmer's spurious victory and unearned adulation form the background for the disaster of Crete. The general loss of honor is further underlined by the fact that Ludovic, who committed two murders in the course of his escape from Crete, is subsequently decorated and even commissioned because he brought his party safely to the coast of Africa.

One can readily understand why Waugh's readers were disappointed when he initially decided to leave Guy Crouchback rather inconclusively at the point of his return to England after the fall of Crete. Nevertheless, even at the time *Officers and Gentlemen* was published, when Waugh had said that he thought two volumes instead of three "would do the trick," he added in his brief introduction, "If I keep my faculties I hope to follow the fortunes of the characters through the whole of their war, but these two constitute a whole."

This statement should not be taken as a commitment on Waugh's part that he would finish the trilogy, Mrs. Waugh has commented to me. "He broke it off because he was tired of it at the time. When the trilogy pushed to the forefront of his mind again, he finished it." Indeed, on the dust jacket of the British edition of the third volume, Waugh said he had known all along that "a third volume was needed," but he had not felt "confident" that he could provide it until then.

Unconditional Surrender (1961)

Only after writing *The Ordeal of Gilbert Pinfold* (1957), the biography *Monsignor Ronald Knox* (1959), and a travel book entitled

Tourist in Africa (1960), did Waugh at last decide to round off his trilogy with the additional volume. For one of its central episodes Waugh reached back to a short story called "Compassion" which he published in the *Month* in 1949, before he had even begun working on *Men at Arms*. The existence of this story adds credence to the view that Waugh had envisioned the overall thematic structure as a trilogy from the start. For "Compassion" embodies an episode which Waugh used not in the first novel of the trilogy but in the final pages of the last volume; and when he did insert it into the larger work, he had designed the slot so that the interpolation would fit in almost the exact words he had written more than a decade before. How seriously then can one take Waugh's earlier statement that the first two novels "constitute a whole," when the material of the short story — without which the trilogy would have remained to some extent thematically unresolved — was waiting in the wings?

"*Men at Arms* began with its hero inspired by illusion, *Officers and Gentlemen* ends with his deflation," Waugh wrote in introducing the latter volume. The third novel begins two years later, in 1943, with Guy on his fortieth birthday contemplating the disappointment his military career has been. In a poignant passage that does not appear in *Sword of Honor* he reflects further about the last four years of his life: "Half an hour's scramble on the beach near Dakar; an ignominious rout in Crete. That had been his war."

Of the two intervening years that have passed since the end of *Officers and Gentlemen* we know only that Guy "remained with his regiment." He sums up his years of service by saying forlornly that "it was not for this that he had dedicated himself on the sword of Roger of Waybroke that hopeful morning four years back."

In the third volume of the trilogy another sword enters the narrative to contrast with Sir Roger's: the sword of Stalingrad, displayed in Westminster Abbey as Britain's gift to the people of Russia. Long lines of people come to see it. The irony implied in

Waugh's use of religious vocabulary in this passage is surely intentional:

> The sword they had come to see stood upright between two candles, on a table counterfeiting an altar. . . . The gossip-writer of the *Daily Express* suggested it should be sent round the kingdom. . . . Now, back from its tour, it reached its apotheosis, exposed for adoration hard by the shrine of St. Edward the Confessor and the sacring place of the kings of England.

To Guy the sword of Stalingrad is the symbol of England's dishonorable alliance with Russia. It reminds the disreputable Ludovic of his own officer's saber, called a state sword, no longer issued as part of an officer's gear — since, Waugh implies, the code of honor it was intended to symbolize no longer exists. When Ludovic mentions his state sword at a party to one of the guests, she says in surprise, "That was a long time ago. Think of it; *swords*."

Since Communist sympathizers are no longer looked upon with suspicion by the government, a little band of British Communists is able to infiltrate the army at various levels. Most of them are homosexuals like their leader Sir Ralph Brompton, who seems "a figure of obsolescent light comedy rather than of total war." For example, Sir Ralph refers affectionately to one of his coterie as "a dear boy and a stalwart party member." Ludovic had spent five years as Sir Ralph's "protégé" and no doubt learned some of his duplicity from his mentor. Sir Ralph arranges to have his fellow homosexual and Communist Everard Spruce publish Ludovic's jottings in Everard's journal, *Survival*, which is dedicated to "the Survival of Values" — a curious theme for a magazine edited by a man who staunchly believes that "the human race is destined to dissolve in chaos." With his customary resourcefulness, Sir Ralph makes sure the magazine is circulated to all branches of the armed forces.

Although Waugh uses Sir Ralph and his group as a basis for satire, serious undertones mark their portrayal, since these men are Waugh's index of the fact that intrigue and betrayal are taken more and more for granted as integrity and honor come to be in ever shorter supply. To Guy's chagrin, even one of the officers who had been trained with him, Frank de Souza, has joined Sir Ralph's group. In what the *Times Literary Supplement* calls Waugh's "stiffening disapproval" of Communism, Waugh has deleted from *Sword of Honor* the reference to the military decoration de Souza was described as having merited in the original version of *Unconditional Surrender.*

Guy finally receives some consolation when the Fascist regime in Italy falls. He hopes that the papacy can now regain the prestige it lost in making the Lateran Treaty with Mussolini. Guy's father, however, insists that the Catholic church does not need worldly prestige: "That isn't at all what the Church is like. It isn't what she's *for.*" He later explains himself to Guy in a letter, referring to the Church by the same term Helena used:

> The Mystical Body doesn't strike attitudes and stand on its dignity. It accepts suffering and injustice. It is ready to forgive at the first hint of compunction. When you spoke of the Lateran Treaty did you consider how many souls may have been reconciled and have died at peace as the result of it? How many children may have been brought up in the faith who might have lived in ignorance? But quantitative judgments don't apply. If only one soul was saved that is full compensation for any amount of loss of "face."

These words of his father have profound effect on Guy when he remembers them at Mr. Crouchback's funeral some months later. To Guy, his father was "the only entirely good man he had ever known." Guy directs his prayers at the funeral to, rather than for, his father as he recalls how his father watched him grow from a happy child "into the lonely captain of Halberdiers who followed the coffin." Almost as if his father's spiritual intercession for him is having immediate results, Guy gets an insight into the nature of his spiritual sloth. He realizes that his attitude toward the service of God has always been one of "reporting for duty" and saying to God in effect, "I don't ask anything from you. . . . I don't suppose I can be of any use, but if there is anything I can do, let me know." Now Guy reflects that this attitude has fostered his *accidia:*

"I don't ask anything from you"; that was the deadly core of his apathy; his father had tried to tell him, was now telling him. . . . In the recesses of Guy's conscience there lay the belief that somewhere, somehow, something would be required of him; that he must be attentive to the summons when it came. . . . One day he would get the chance to do some small service which only he could perform, for which he had been created. Even he must have his function in the divine plan. He did not expect a heroic destiny. Quantitative judgments did not apply. All that mattered was to recognize the chance when it was offered. Perhaps his father was at that moment clearing the way for him. "Show me what to do and help me to do it," he prayed.

Waugh is here applying to Guy what he had considered the lesson of St. Helena's life: that God wants a different thing from each person, "laborious or easy, conspicuous or quite private, but something which only we can do and for which we were created."[95] This principle is to work itself out in Guy's life in ways Guy cannot now foresee. The first opportunity in which he emerges as apparently the only one able to save the situation involves his ex-wife Virginia. She has become pregnant with Trimmer's child and has made every effort to have an abortion — a difficult task in wartime London: "It was Fate. For weeks now she had been haunted by the belief that in a world devoted to destruction and slaughter this one odious life was destined to survive."

Meanwhile Guy, who is going through parachute training in preparation for joining a special mission to Yugoslavia, injures his knee in a fall. Temporarily incapacitated, he returns to London on leave and is thus available to remarry Virginia for the sake of the child and also in order to provide himself with an heir. Kerstie Kilbannock, Ian's wife, criticizes Guy for playing the knight errant: "Can't you understand men aren't chivalrous any more and I don't believe they ever were." Guy replies:

"Knights errant . . . used to go out looking for noble deeds. I don't think I've ever in my life done a single, positively unselfish action. I certainly haven't gone out of my way to find opportunities. Here was something most unwelcome, put into my hands; something which I believe the Americans describe as 'beyond the call of duty'; not the normal behavior of an officer and a gentleman; something they'll laugh about in Bellamy's."

Guy continues that he is aware half the population of Europe is homeless and that he knows he cannot do anything about all of them. "This is just one case where I can help. And only I, really." He is in a position to consider the soul of a child who would otherwise have no chance of survival "born unwanted in 1944." Later Guy reaffirms to himself his father's words, "Quantitative judgments don't apply. If only one soul was saved, that is full compensation for any amount of loss of 'face.'" He would not expect Kerstie to understand this. Here is Waugh's own interpretation of this episode:

> I imply that there is a moral purpose, a chance of salvation, in every human life. Do you know the old Protestant hymn which goes: "Once to every man and nation/ Comes the moment to decide"? Guy is offered this chance by making himself responsible for the upbringing of Trimmer's child, to see that he is not brought up by his dissolute mother. He is essentially an unselfish character.[96]

But surprisingly enough, Virginia is on the verge of trying to mend her ways. She had originally decided to become a Roman Catholic to entice Guy into remarrying her. Though she now realizes that Guy will remarry her in any case, she has decided to accept the Catholic religion nonetheless because she recognizes how empty the last fifteen years of her life have been.

As she ends the period of her religious instruction, Virginia remarks, "It's all so easy. . . . I can't think what those novelists make such a fuss over — about people 'losing their faith.' The whole thing is clear as daylight to me. I wonder why no one ever told me before." Later she makes her first confession and is entranced by the idea that "the same words were said to her as were said to Guy. The same grace was offered. Little Trimmer stirred as she knelt at the side-altar and pronounced the required penance."

Even Guy's eccentric Uncle Peregrine, who up to this point — in one of Waugh's personal jokes on himself — has found it "difficult to regard converts as Catholics," must admit that "Virginia has taken to religion in an extraordinary way." Extraordinary, at any rate, for Virginia. Peregrine does not try to explain her behavior, since he has always preferred to leave such things "in higher hands." But the reader sees clearly that Virginia, to at least some extent, has felt "the twitch upon the thread" by which God drew to Himself the central characters of *Brideshead Revisited* (one of those novels in which there is "such a fuss" made over people "losing their faith").

Virginia's baby, Gervase, is born on 4 June 1944, the day Rome is liberated by the Allies. For his part Guy, who has already returned to active duty, is content that the sole heir to the Crouchback name is alive and well. He is no longer *fin de ligne,* the end of his family's line, as he had been referred to more than once at his father's funeral.

Guy has been posted to Yugoslavia as part of a mission to aid Marshal Tito's partisans against the Germans. En route Guy's plane crashes, just as Waugh recounts in his diary that his plane did. Waugh remembered circling the field in preparation for landing but, like Guy, had no recollection of the crash itself: "The next thing I knew was that I was walking in a cornfield by the light of a burning airplane," talking to a strange British officer. (16 July 1944).

Upon his arrival in Yugoslavia Guy, who has not been able to shake his abiding depression for more than brief periods, is told that the officer whom he succeeded had "fallen into melancholy" and had to be recalled. Because of Guy's antipathy for Communism in every form, including that espoused by the partisans, he foresees a like depression casting its shadow over him.

Guy's ill will toward the partisans was shared fully by his creator. Lord Birkenhead, who served with Waugh in Yugoslavia, recalls that Waugh avoided meeting the Communist officer attached to the British mission there "by leaving the room whenever this man entered it."[97]

Guy's hostility for the Communists is further strengthened when the partisans allow Ritchie-Hook to die in an attack on the enemy; Guy does not know the attack was a sham, engineered to impress a visiting American general. For critic Paul Doyle this is "one of the most ironic scenes in modern fiction." Doyle continues, "Representing the courageous values and deeds of the old Britain, Ritchie-Hook dies fighting heroically while Communist partisan cowardice and a politically motivated group of British military figures look on and behave with caddish and cowardly duplicity."[98]

Guy is desolate throughout his entire stay in Yugoslavia. His unhappiness is compounded when his sister Angela writes him that both Virgina and Peregrine have been killed in an air raid. Providentially (or would Virginia have called it Fate?) the baby was staying with Angela. "In a world devoted to destruction and slaughter," this one life has indeed begun to seem "destined to survive," as Virginia had said before the baby was born.

After Virginia's death Guy recalls the weeks they lived together after their remarriage; as his knee mended "the deep old wound" in his heart and pride healed too. Guy is gradually overcoming his spiritual discouragement and receives yet another opportunity to help others which will enable him to make further progress. While in Yugoslavia he comes across a band of Jewish refugees. They have been wandering ever since their release from a German concentration camp. Now they are at the mercy of the anti-Semitic Communist partisans, who are not interested in helping them leave Yugoslavia. Guy realizes that once more he has been given the chance to help others who seem to have no other recourse, as he had helped Virginia and her unborn child.

This is the episode which first appeared as the short story "Compassion," published in 1949. The character who is to become Guy Crouchback is a Scotsman named Major Gordon. The story fits perfectly into the trilogy, where Guy reflects that "in a world of hate and waste" he is being offered another chance of doing "a single small act to redeem the times." Or, as the straightforward Major Gordon puts it, he finally has a chance to do something "worth while in this bloody war."[99]

Guy doggedly cuts through the red tape which bars the Jews from leaving Yugoslavia. He feels like "Moses leading a people out of captivity" when, on his forty-first birthday, he finally obtains all the necessary permissions. However, Guy is shaken out of whatever complacency he might have been tempted to feel by Mme. Kanyi, one of the refugees, who with her husband has acted as liaison between Guy and the Jews. Mme. Kanyi unwittingly leads Guy to realize that he is making reparation for the attitude with which he went to war when she muses:

> "Is there any place that is free from evil? It is too simple to say that only the Nazis wanted war. . . . It seems to me there was a will to war, a death wish, everywhere. Even good men thought their private honor would be satisfied by war. They could assert their manhood by killing and being killed. They would accept hardships in recompense for having been selfish and lazy. Danger justified privilege. I knew Italians — not very many perhaps — who felt this. Were there none in England?" "God forgive me," said Guy. "I was one of them."

Guy too had welcomed the war as a chance to vindicate his honor and purge his soul, just as Alastair Trumpington in *Put Out More Flags* joined the army because "he'd never done anything for his country" and wanted to do "a kind of penance" for his purposeless life up to that time.

The Jews are finally allowed to leave Yugoslavia only to be billeted in a valley in Italy behind barbed wire, since the authorities do not know what else to do with them. At least they are no longer being persecuted. But even this minor victory is blighted for Guy by tragedy. He is shattered to learn from one of Sir Ralph Brompton's agents that Mme. Kanyi and her husband have been liquidated by the partisans on trumped-up charges as a reprisal for their dealings with him in getting the Jews out of Yugoslavia. Guy himself is being recalled to England at the behest of the partisans. The pattern of Guy's army career has thus held firm to the last, as critic Herbert Howarth remarks: anything brave or competent or humane which Guy managed to accomplish has always been recorded in the official dossiers to his discredit.[100]

In the short story Major Gordon discusses the fate of the Kanyis with the chaplain and another officer. "You did all you could. A darn sight more than most people would have done," the officer tells Gordon. "That's your answer," the chaplain adds. "You mustn't judge actions by their apparent success. Everything you did was good in itself." Even though it seems that Major Gordon's actions did not help the Kanyis, the chaplain suggests that what Gordon tried to do for them has done Gordon himself some good. "No suffering need ever be wasted. It is just as much part of Charity to receive cheerfully as to give."

Guy Crouchback is offered no such consolation, although Waugh has otherwise incorporated the short story into the novel almost verbatim. Instead Guy is overwhelmed by a sense of futility:

> He had come to the end of the crusade to which he had devoted himself on the tomb of Sir Roger. His life as a Halberdier was over. All the stamping on the barracks square and the biffing of imaginary strongholds were finding their consummation in one frustrated act of mercy.

Guy consequently leaves Yugoslavia for England at the end of 1944 knowing that his career in the army is just about over. On the surface he has nothing to be particularly proud of as far as the official records have recorded his career. But this no longer matters to Guy, who finally realizes that the prayer he uttered at his father's funeral has been answered. He has been able to help others in circumstances in which he was the only one who could or would take action — both in the case of Virginia and in the case of the Jewish refugees. Guy has come to accept the fact that "no good comes from public causes; only private causes of the soul," as Waugh himself comments.[101] This lesson has been so impressed on Guy's nephew Tony Box-Bender that Tony decides to enter a monastery when he is released from the army. Tony's decision indicates the respect which Waugh had for the contemplative life, a respect clearly evidenced in Waugh's nonfiction and his correspondence with Thomas Merton. As Waugh wrote rather caustically in *Commonweal*, "I believe that we are returning to a stage when on the supernatural plane only heroic prayer can save us, and when on the natural plane the cloister offers a saner and more civilized life than 'the world'" (11 March 1949).

Although Waugh looked upon the monastic life as a very special vocation, something of withdrawal from the world is implied in Guy's retiring after the war to live in the country, insulated from the hostile and disordered world beyond the gates of Broome. An epilogue which takes place in June 1951 reveals that Guy has married a girl named Domenica Plessington and settled down to a serene life at Broome.

Domenica very much resembles Cordelia, the youngest Marchmain in *Brideshead Revisited*. Before meeting Guy, Domenica had tried to settle herself in a convent, failed, and then took to working on the family farm, where she could be found "trousered, muddied, and full of the rough jargon of the stockyard." As Arthur Box-Bender, Guy's brother-in-law, explains to a crony of his at his Club: Domenica's mother, Eloise, looked after the baby when Guy was abroad; Domenica got very fond of it. "A marriage was the obvious thing. I think Eloise deserves some credit in arranging it. Domenica manages the home farm at Broome."

By the end of *Sword of Honor* it seems that Providence has at last worked things out in Guy's favor, though not quite as generously as at the end of the third novel of the trilogy, where Arthur Box-Bender says, "Now they've two boys of their own."

On the last page of *Sword of Honor*, Waugh denies Guy offspring of his own, for he has Box-Bender say instead, "Pity they haven't any children of their own." The *Times Literary Supplement* therefore concludes, "The happy, lucky ending is for some reason no longer acceptable. Mr. Waugh's picture of Divine Providence has been seriously altered."[102]

I disagree. The revised version of the trilogy makes clear that if Virginia's son by Trimmer had not survived her attempts at abortion and the bomb that killed her, and if Guy had not accepted the child as his own, Guy would have had no heir to perpetuate the Crouchback name. Laura Waugh explained to me that Waugh deleted from the epilogue any suggestion of Guy's having children of his own "because he wanted to reinforce the fact that Guy had married Domenica as an act of generosity, to provide a home for her and for Virginia's child."

Since little Gervase is Guy's "first born," he is Guy's heir, whether or not Guy has any more children. Hence, when Guy decided to remarry Virginia, he in effect unselfishly willed the Crouchback name and all that went with it to the son of Trimmer. One is reminded of Mme. Kanyi's words to Guy, "It is not always true that suffering makes people unselfish. But sometimes it is." At the conclusion of the trilogy Guy seems at long last to have overcome the temptation to spiritual sloth which has dogged him throughout his adult life. The overcoming of this temptation has led Guy to unselfish charity and generosity toward others.

For all the serious notes struck in *Sword of Honor*, Waugh has not lost his sense of humor. The last we hear of Ludovic is that he seems to have fallen into romantic illusions similar to those with which Guy started out. He has even bought the Castello Crouchback in Santa Dulcina, where Guy had lived in isolation for eight years before the war. There Ludovic lives with a homosexual companion, an American named Padfield, whom he met through Sir Ralph's circle. Ludovic has written a best-selling novel, *The Death Wish*, which is "a very gorgeous, almost gaudy, tale of romance and high drama." This puts Ludovic in the mainstream with the popular novelists who are composing books which "turn from the drab alleys of the thirties into the odorous gardens of a recent past transformed and illuminated by disordered memory and imagination."

Here Waugh is satirizing *Brideshead Revisited*, for the death scene which Ludovic plans for Lady Marmaduke Transept is a parody of Lord Marchmain's death in *Brideshead*. Ludovic, Waugh implies in still another joke on himself, has become romantic enough to write a *Brideshead Revisited*. Gore Vidal finds Waugh's witty satirical thrusts one of the trilogy's saving graces. In the *New York Times Book Review* he cites such "splendid acts of destruction" as Guy's impressions of Winston Churchill's wartime broadcasts:

> Guy had found them painfully boastful and they had, most of them, been immediately followed by the news of some disaster, as though in retribution from the God of Kipling's *Recessional*.

"Juvenal was amiable to Domitian by comparison," says Vidal. He goes on to refer to Waugh's satire of *Brideshead* in Ludovic's *Death Wish* with lines that are a tribute to Waugh: "Waugh has turned the full glare of his cold eye upon himself. . . . A satirist capable of self-scrutiny breaks new ground. . . . His military trilogy has much to recommend it. The wit endures; at full strength, wit is rage made bearable, and useful" (7 January 1962).

Consequently, although the one-volume version of the trilogy is perhaps handier than three separate books, the gain in compactness and the few felicitous additions it offers are not enough. They do not compensate for the sacrifice of many delightfully witty passages, some of which I have pointed out. Large helpings of Waugh's wit are still to be found in the revised edition. They help to lighten — not neutralize — the serious tone of a story which, because of its theme, would otherwise be very somber indeed. In addition, they serve to anchor the religious dimension of the story solidly in the context of the human comedy and thus help to insure that the spiritual experience reflected in the novel is also a very human one.

By the time Waugh wrote the trilogy, he had learned to refine his comic flair according to the demands of serious fiction. In fact, the religious theme of *Sword of Honor* is perfectly integrated with plot and character in a blend that Waugh had not achieved since *Brideshead Revisited*. Like Helena, Guy is aware of his relationship to God and the demands which this makes on him as God's creature with a defined purpose — Waugh's announced theme for his later fiction. In *Helena*, this religious theme predominated in a way that seemed to subordinate plot and characterization. But in the trilogy, the religious implications are part of the total fabric of a story which works just as successfully on the level of technique as it does on the level of theme.

Critic Andrew Rutherford finds that in Waugh's hands the full potential of the trilogy as a literary form has been realized:

> Each novel records a distinct phase in the hero's emotional, spiritual, and military progress; each contributes to the elaborate patterning of events, of recurring and contrasting motifs, which characterizes the trilogy as a whole. The resulting sense of unity in diversity is so satisfying, aesthetically and thematically, that one is tempted to speculate on the unique felicity of tripartite division in complex works of art.[103]

Perhaps the most interesting facet of Waugh's achievement in the trilogy is the way he has transmuted his own experience in the service into the fabric of his fiction. John St. John has recalled for the *London Times* having served in the same regiment with Waugh during the war. To him Waugh's observation of army life is "meticulous and completely honest." For example, Waugh himself was involved in an attempt to save a group of Jewish refugees interned in Yugoslavia. This episode developed in a fashion very similar to that of the episode he describes in *Sword of Honor*. St. John concludes his remarks about Waugh's use of his wartime experience with a statement that sums up the material in St. John's subsequent book, *To the War with Waugh:*

> His characters are fictional but anyone who served with him has no difficulty in putting a name to Brigadier Ritchie-Hook, to Apthorpe, Trimmer and the rest. The incidents as well as the men in

the books are taken from life. . . . The Highland regiment embarked by mistake on the Halberdiers' troopship at Liverpool was in fact the Eighth Argyll and Sutherlands; his account of the shooting of deer with tommy-guns actually took place, not on the Isle of Mugg but at Inverary; the fiasco of Crouchback's expedition to West Africa is near-history. . . . Evelyn's novels are a splendid antidote to the glamorized . . . version of the 1939-45 war that is now the mode. They provide the truest, as well as the funniest, guide to the war as I knew it. (7 September 1969)

Because Waugh has so lavishly filled in all of the details on his broad canvas, the trilogy resists easy translation to another medium. The 1967 BBC-TV presentation of *Sword of Honor* (in three ninety-five-minute segments) was a "glorious failure," according to one critic, because the subtleties of character and motivation in the original proved inseparable from the subtleties of Waugh's writing; the characters and their actions became oversimplified.

Upon viewing the TV version of *Sword of Honor* in its entirety through the kindness of BBC-TV, however, I personally found that a surprising amount of the subtlety of Waugh's work had been preserved in Giles Cooper's literate TV script. Waugh looked the script over, said Mrs. Waugh, and seemed pleased with it. The series was screened only a few months after Waugh's death in January 1967 and repeated that December. Cooper used much of the original dialogue from the novels and was at pains to include material that pertained to the theme as well as the plot, such as Guy's reflections at Mr. Crouchback's funeral and Ludovic's speech about his state sword. Indeed Cooper had the happy thought of ending the trilogy with Ludovic's gazing at the tomb of Sir Roger in precisely the manner Guy did at the beginning of the first TV segment, indicating that Ludovic has fallen heir to Guy's discarded illusions.

The television presentation of *Sword of Honor* prompted new interest in the trilogy in England. Both Waugh's son Auberon and daughter Harriet feel that eventually the trilogy will be recognized as Evelyn Waugh's best work. "At the time of my father's death," adds Teresa D'Arms, "the better critics were already taking it more seriously than they had before, as evidenced by the number of times that the trilogy was cited in obituaries."

One important work of Waugh's remains to be discussed: *The Ordeal of Gilbert Pinfold*. In this curious book Waugh the novelist and Waugh the man are even more closely allied than they were in the *Sword of Honor* trilogy. Indeed, if Guy Crouchback is a fictional portrait of Waugh in the war years, Gilbert Pinfold is a fictional portrait of Waugh as he was after the war up to the end of his life, living much as Waugh lived and thinking much as Waugh thought.

7

Conclusion: A Little Hope

Waugh pictures himself in his postwar years in *The Ordeal of Gilbert Pinfold* (1957), the most autobiographical of his novels. Gilbert Pinfold was in fact the name of a former owner of Waugh's home, Piers Court — an indication of Waugh's wish to identify himself with the character of Pinfold. Judging from the tenor of his nonfiction during these years, this fictionalized description approaches the way Waugh saw himself:

> The Pinfolds were Roman Catholic, Mrs. Pinfold by upbringing, Mr. Pinfold by a later development. . . . At the very time when the leaders of his Church were exhorting their people to emerge from the catacombs into the forum, to make their influence felt in democratic politics and to regard worship as a corporate rather than a private act, Mr. Pinfold burrowed ever deeper into the rock.

Waugh clearly considered himself a Catholic writer in the sense that he felt his early religious training and eventual conversion did much to shape his outlook on life as expressed in his writings. "I deal in human experience, and becoming a Catholic opened a whole new field of experience to me," he explained to an interviewer, Thomas Ryan. "As a novelist dealing in human experience the very essence of my work is colored by my beliefs, and it would be foolish to claim I was not a Catholic writer."[104]

By this statement, however, Waugh did not mean that he sought to impose religious ideas on his work; rather he meant that his religious frame of reference was an integral part of his fiction. This is evident when one reads the statements Waugh made about what it means to be a Catholic writer. Some of the best of these statements appear in his reviews of the novels of Graham Greene. Indeed, Waugh's criticism of Greene's fiction often tells us as much about Waugh as it does about Greene.

For example, in reviewing Greene's *End of the Affair*, Waugh praises Greene's "defiant assertion of the supernatural," yet suggests tactfully that Greene might appear sectarian in his handling of certain parts of the story. While on the one hand the novel presents the Catholic church "as something in their midst mysterious and triumphant and working for their good," on the other hand there is the matter of the heroine's baptism. As is learned after her death, she had been baptized by a Catholic priest. Some speculate whether or not "it took." Waugh comments:

> But Mr. Greene knows very well that she would have been as surely baptized by the local vicar. It would be a pity if he gave an impression of the Catholic Church as a secret society. . . . Clearly that is not Mr. Greene's intention nor can it be justly read into his words, but in the dark places where his apostolate lies I can imagine some passages carrying a whiff of occultism (17 August 1951).

Obviously, then, Waugh felt that a novelist must avoid being "parochial" in expressing his religious convictions in his work. He tried to embed the religious dimension of his novels within the substance of the fiction itself. What Waugh says of Pinfold in a sentence added to the American edition of the novel was therefore true of himself: "He was sometimes referred to as a leading Catholic but his leadership was not conspicuous."

Becoming more and more self-revealing, Waugh–Pinfold admits that his strongest tastes are negative. He abhors plastics, jazz, and everything else that has happened during his lifetime. He continues:

> The tiny kindling of charity which came to him through his religion sufficed to temper his disgust and change it to boredom. . . .
> At intervals during the day and night he would look at his watch and learn always with disappointment how little of his life was past, how much there was still ahead of him. He wished no one ill, but he looked at the world *sub specie aeternitatis* ["in the light of eternity"] and he found it flat as a map; except, when, rather often, personal annoyance intruded.

English poet James Kirkup remembers an occasion when he became the object of Waugh's "personal annoyance" through picking wild flowers along a narrow country lane which, unknown to him, was Waugh's property. Waugh's quick anger at discovering an interloper just as quickly disappeared when he found that Kirkup was "a man of letters," and he amiably invited him in for a sherry.[105]

Waugh occasionally emerged from his country home, not only for afternoon trips to the cinema in nearby Dursley but also for longer excursions, such as his trip to Hollywood in 1947 to confer with MGM about the filming of *Brideshead Revisited*. Shortly after the publication of *Helena* in 1950 he was made a Companion of Literature by royal appointment. Waugh began his war trilogy at Piers Court and continued working on it after he had moved to equally remote Combe Florey in Somerset, where he lived the last decade of his life.

In the introductory chapter I pointed out that from the values incorporated by a novelist into his fiction the reader can build a picture of the author's *persona* — the totality of attitudes and opinions which the author implies to be his own. This *persona* or implied author may not correspond entirely to the outlook of the real author, for a novelist can assume a pose in his writing which does not completely express his own point of view. In the case of

Waugh, as critic J. M. Cameron writes in his obituary in
Commonweal:

> He early chose to exhibit to the world a *persona* in accordance with
> which he was taken to be the champion of a dying aristocratic cul-
> ture and the enemy of the vulgarities of the new democratic
> world. This *persona* was not only put on for the occasional public
> pronouncement: it seemed also to be worn by the novelist, or at
> least by those of his heroes, such as Charles Ryder of *Brideshead
> Revisited* and Guy Crouchback of the novels of the Second World
> War, with whom it seemed plausible to identify the author. (29
> April 1966)

Waugh's *persona* had broader implications than those Cameron
enumerates and can best be summed up by focusing on Waugh's
hostility to the modern age. This hostility runs through his
diaries and other nonfiction as well as his fiction. In fact a comparison of Waugh's fiction and nonfiction demonstrates how
close the *persona* of Waugh the novelist was to the personal vision
of Waugh the man.

"The first obvious gush of anti-Modernism in my father's fiction is manifested in *Handful of Dust,*" says Auberon Waugh, "in
passages such as the one in which Tony Last is repelled by the
'chromium world' of Mrs. Beaver, the interior decorator," which
reflects the ugly world of sterile chaos Tony feels is engulfing the
values he cherishes. "For my father Modernism could best be defined as the glorification of the Modern Age as the way things
should be." "More than any of his works," Thomas Staley remarks in *Commonweal,* "*A Handful of Dust* reveals Waugh's position
in the mainstream of modern fiction, and reflects . . . a vision
which he shared in common with any number of modern writers
from D. H. Lawrence to Albert Camus" (27 May 1966). Tony
Last cannot cope with the new order because he has lost contact
with the cultural and religious heritage which would enable him
to deal with it.

Charles Ryder, on the other hand, reestablishes his link with
the past by accepting the Catholic faith, thereby implying that

man must have *some* values which are meaningful to him if he is to be truly human. Rex Mottram (Julia's ex-husband) and Hooper (Charles's subordinate officer) are ridiculed by Waugh not because they are non-Catholics but because they are totally unaware of any dimension of reality transcending the natural level on which they operate. They are thus aimless and materialistic. So are many of the characters in *The Loved One*, which Cyril Connolly characterized as a study of "the elaborate effort made by those who most worship comfort, beauty and life to euphemize that stark object which is of all the most ill-favored and unreassuring. In its attitude to death, and to death's stand-in, failure, Mr. Waugh exposes a materialistic society at its weakest spot, as would Swift or Donne were they alive today."[106]

Even *Helena*, Waugh's only historical novel, is a veiled attack on the modern age, for Helena is pictured as having to cope with the modern age of her day, the decadent Roman society which she sees mirrored in her erratic son Constantine and his court. But Waugh's most savage satirical attack on modern times is *Love among the Ruins*, in which he criticizes (perhaps too obviously) the disappearance of Christian humanism from the western world.

The Ordeal of Gilbert Pinfold (1957)

In his semi-autobiographical novel *The Ordeal of Gilbert Pinfold*, Waugh restates his conviction that the artist can best deal with the modern world by establishing an independent system of order and withdrawing if necessary from commerce with secular life. Upon leaving his secluded country home and venturing into the chaotic world beyond, Pinfold finds his hold on Christian values imperiled when he is apparently persecuted by a group of people who reject his ideals.

He sets out on a trip to Colombo, Ceylon. At sea he begins to experience what he only afterwards recognizes as hallucinations brought on by an overdose of medicine. Pinfold believes himself persecuted by a whole family on board his ship; their disembodied voices accuse him in exaggerated fashion of all the faults for which he has ever been criticized. His novels, he is told, are marked by "morbid sentimentality; gross and hackneyed farce, alternating with grosser and more hackneyed melodrama." His religious profession, he learns, is "humbug, assumed in order to ingratiate himself with the aristocracy," since not a few of the titled families in England have a Catholic background. "The charges," critic Malcolm Bradbury points out, "have a savage accuracy, being a corrupt version of his own self-image."[107]

As Pinfold's journey into fantasy progresses, his ship becomes a microcosm of the whole secularized world he has sought to escape. He learns, for example, that there is no clergyman on board and that a layman conducts the weekly nonconformist service. When one of the crew dies in Pinfold's fantasy, he finds that the funeral is held on the sports deck, "the most likely place for the ceremony," since it is carried out in a perfunctory fashion hardly worthy of a Christian burial service. Eventually Pinfold's own religious practices begin to slip. "He had given up any attempt at saying his prayers; the familiar hallowed words provoked a storm of blasphemous parody" from his persecutors.

That the ship has become for Pinfold the incarnation of the godless contemporary world is emphasized by the fact that once he has landed in Colombo, he immediately goes off to mass at the local Catholic church. So virtue triumphs. Finally Pinfold reaches England once more. He wires his wife to meet him in London and escort him back to his country home, just as Waugh did. In a short time Pinfold is sufficiently recovered from his ordeal to set down his experiences in fictional form. He puts aside the novel on which he was working before he went on his cruise (in reality Waugh's *Unconditional Surrender*, the third novel of the *Sword of Honor* trilogy) and begins to work on *The Ordeal of Gilbert Pinfold*.

This novel reflects an unsettling experience that happened to Waugh in much the manner he describes in the book.

Waugh suffered from insomnia (as well as depression) in his

later years. For a time he tried taking unmeasured doses of chloral, a sleep-inducing compound, which he mixed with crème de menthe to make it more appetizing. "Evelyn liked to drink, but not to excess," Father D'Arcy remarks. "But the medicine which he was taking for his insomnia did not mix well with alcohol or with the medicine which he was taking for other ailments such as rheumatism; as a result he was for a time the victim of the hallucinations during a voyage to Ceylon which he described in *Gilbert Pinfold*. He was attacked by these hallucinations while he was travelling. Laura Waugh called Farm Street Church from the Hyde Park Hotel in London where she had gone to meet Evelyn after his return from his journey in the hope that I could come and see him. I was away at the time and so Father Philip Caraman, whom I had introduced to the Waughs earlier, went round to see them. He found Evelyn very disturbed and talking to himself during dinner. So he rang up a psychiatrist, Dr. Eric Strauss, who gave Evelyn a sedative after talking to him about the hallucinations from which he had suffered while he was away. Dr. Strauss's prescription immediately cured him of them, but Evelyn afterward liked to joke about this experience as the time when he had gone mad."[108]

Some literary critics have wondered whether a case history of delusions can really be considered fiction. In fact *Pinfold* is important to the corpus of Waugh's work not merely as another piece of fiction but as a perfect extension of the religious vision which permeates Waugh's later works. Even though Pinfold eventually recognizes his delusions for what they are, he nonetheless finds it difficult while under their influence to champion the serious themes of his fiction and the personal convictions underlying them against a world which rejects his ideals. The only solution for Pinfold is to remain at home where he can live by his own value system, secure from the demoralizing influence of the antagonistic and disordered world outside his citadel. Like Helena, Pinfold knows his destiny. He knows that his mission is to reassert in his fiction the ideals by which he lives and thus to remind modern man of Christian values in a post-Christian world.

The trilogy begins where *Pinfold* leaves off; the hero, a Catholic gentleman, is living in isolation according to a certain set of religious and social ideals — those Guy Crouchback sees epitomized in his father. Guy strives to become a man like his father and in his own way at last succeeds when he conceives the idea of serving his fellowmen by personal charity rather than by public exploits as a soldier. This seems to him (and to Waugh) to be the only way a man of honor can cope with the modern age without losing personal integrity.

A reader need not accept Waugh's personal view of life, however, in order to enjoy Waugh's fiction. If a novelist succeeds only in enshrining his own views in his work, he can be appreciated only by those who share them, and his work cannot endure. If on the other hand he has caught some aspects of the human predicament in his fiction, as Waugh certainly has, his novels transcend the particular period and problems they treat.

The function of the artist is not to offer clear-cut answers to the human problems with which he deals but to present them in a provocative way. He leads the reader to consider them for himself, to find his own solutions within his own frame of reference. Theologian Hubert Van Zeller tells the story of a hurried airport interview Waugh gave in New York. A reporter asked Waugh if he agreed with Will Rogers that the purpose of art is not to make men think but to make them happy. Waugh asked in return, "This Mr. Rogers is dead, is he not?" Upon being assured that he was, Waugh replied, "In that case he knows better now."[109]

Waugh's novels do stir the reader to think about the problems confronting anyone concerned about man's relationship to God and to the modern age. But Waugh is not necessarily saying that Guy Crouchback's way of solving this problem, by withdrawing to what is left of the family estate and continuing to serve God in a private capacity by caring for his immediate family, is the *only* solution. Guy's personality makes his choice understandable.

Waugh's personality makes understandable his choice of much the same course in later life, duplicated by his surrogate Mr. Pinfold. But Waugh continued to admire Helena, who chose to meet the modern age of her time head-on. As Rutherford has remarked in summing up his essay on *Sword of Honor:*

> A writer's prejudices, like his obsessions, are indeed a reservoir of power. Uncontrolled, they limit his achievement; carefully exploited, they enhance it; challenged and transcended, they can convert it into major art. Waugh's trilogy presents a uniquely successful fusion of prejudice indulged with prejudices overcome, as the vision that seemed by its very nature static shows itself continually capable of change and growth. That Guy's final position (or Waugh's) is not our own need not disturb us, for it is the intensity of the process as much as the conclusions reached that gives it its validity, wins our respect, and earns the hero his right to a wryly unconventional happy ending.[110]

In his obituary of Waugh in the *Tablet* Douglas Woodruff, who knew him for many years, has movingly described Waugh's frame of mind in his last years.

> He found himself more and more out of sympathy with the world as it developed on both sides of the Atlantic, and in the last five years he was saddened by developments in the Church which seemed to him to reflect parallel tendencies. . . . In the last letter he wrote to this paper . . . he reflected a very general feeling of dismay among those who were instructed and received into the Church thirty or forty years previously, and had been given a very different account of what they were joining and what they were leaving behind. . . . Father D'Arcy, who had instructed him and whom he continued to regard as the cleverest man he had known, could not induce a more cheerful outlook. (16 April 1966)

In his diary notation for Easter Sunday 1965, Waugh commented, "A year in which the process of transforming the liturgy has followed a planned course. Protests avail nothing. . . . I shall not live to see things righted." Waugh's concern about changes in the Catholic church was symptomatic of the overall despondency which marked his last years. He did not look to the future with optimism. "Only when one has lost all curiosity about the future has one reached the age to write an autobiography," he said at the beginning of *A Little Learning.* "The future, dreariest of prospects."[111]

"At the end of his life," Father D'Arcy recalls, "Evelyn was going through a bad period. He was sleepless and unwell. Everything which he had stood for had gone up in smoke, he thought. The allies had sided with Yugoslavia and Russia, two Communist countries, in World War II. And Vatican II hit him hard. He thought what happened during the Protestant Revolt would happen again. The Protestants had started by putting the mass into the vernacular and ended by abolishing it altogether," a phenomenon which Waugh had treated in his life of Edmund Campion.

Waugh therefore could not bring himself at any time to accept the *aggiornamento* ("renewal") in the Church because he saw it ultimately as a capitulation to the modern age, as I noted in discussing his preface to the one-volume edition of the *Sword of Honor* trilogy. Writing to the *Tablet* he said:

> If the young were filled with ingenuous joy in their own period, I could well understand that it might be desirable to purge the Church of the accretions of antiquity. But, so far as one can judge from the artists, dramatists, novelists, and journalists, the articulate young seem to be obsessed with horror of the modern world. They might well find attraction in an institution which offered them something antithetical to the spirit of the day. (21 September 1963)

Regardless of Waugh's lack of sympathy for the efforts at renewal, "he never, for one moment, lost his allegiance to the Church," Christopher Sykes has written to me. "I remember his saying more than once, 'I shall never be an apostate.' But he certainly suffered a great loss of affection for the Church. He was acutely conscious of the gravity of the first and the relative unimportance of the second. This comes out in many of his letters to his friends, and not just to his Catholic friends."

Throughout his life Waugh was tempted to a discouragement similar to that which he described as afflicting Tony Last, Charles Ryder, Guy Crouchback, Gilbert Pinfold, and all of the other heroes closely identified with his own point of view. This propensity to melancholy boredom increased as Waugh grew older and found the ideals which he had valued all of his life largely ignored. Contemplating in his very last diary entry the death of an old friend, Philip Dunne, Waugh mourned the loss of a man who was truly chivalrous, who possessed "a sense of private honor uncommon nowadays" (Easter Sunday 1965). "The tiny kindling of charity which came to him through his religion," Waugh wrote of his alter ego Gilbert Pinfold, "sufficed only to temper his disgust" with modern life "and change it to boredom."

Sir Arnold Lunn, an acquaintance of Waugh's, has been a great help in showing how this aspect of Waugh's description of Pinfold applies to Waugh himself. He wrote in the *National Review:*

> Waugh could not be described as a happy man. I asked him what he really enjoyed. He replied, "Cessation from pain." He admitted that there were periods when he enjoyed life, but these were offset by periods of increasing boredom. He got very little pleasure out of writing, and even less out of success: . . . "I have that degree of detachment from the world . . . which would be very edifying if it led to love of Christ but is not at all edifying because it merely leads to boredom." (27 February 1968)

To Hubert Van Zeller the cause of Waugh's desolation at this time of his life was his vision of modern man's gradual loss of Christian values and moral standards; Waugh decided that at least he could "keep the march of progress from turning in at his gates."[112] Waugh's cousin Claud Cockburn sees Waugh's use of an ear trumpet in his later years as a symbol of this attitude. This instrument, says Cockburn, seemed larger than any other ear trumpet ever seen, for its function was not simply to assist hearing: "On the contrary, it was to emphasize and portray, in an unmistakable physical manner, the laborious difficulty its owner had in understanding any communication the modern world might be seeking to make to him."[113] Or, as Waugh says in his diary, "One has heard all the world has to say, and wants no more of it" (9 May 1962).

Because of his unhappy frame of mind, Waugh did not write much during his last year. "He was commissioned to write a history of the Crusades," says Teresa Waugh D'Arms, "and he read a great deal on the subject for several months. But he finally gave up the project in weariness and distaste. Fortunately he was able to repay the advance which he had received for the book, which wasn't easy." Waugh's interest in the Holy Land had already produced *Helena*, but he could no longer muster enthusiasm for a long-term project.

Shortly before his death Waugh decided to begin work on the second volume of his autobiography, *A Little Hope*, but he finished only eight pages. Alec Waugh speculates that his brother's inability to deal with the painful period of his divorce may partially explain the writing block that held Evelyn all but inoperative during his last year.[114] To Laura Waugh the reason her husband developed a writing block during his last year seems clear: "I would have thought it obvious that with the changes in the Church he lost all impetus for creative writing." Waugh's published utterances about the changes initiated by Vatican II make hers the most plausible explanation. Some obituaries speculated on what kind of fiction Waugh would have written had he lived, but Harriet Waugh says that he had decided he would write no more fiction after he published the revised trilogy.

Waugh weakened steadily during his last months and saw less and less of even his close friends. One of these, Anthony Powell, who was responsible for getting Waugh's first book published, said in the *New York Times Book Review* that "Evelyn was in a melancholic and wretched state at the end of his life" (9 May 1969). Another friend, Lady Diana Cooper, says, "His cross was too heavy, too immaterial and abstract for him to carry — so he laid it down."[115]

Evelyn Waugh died in his home at Combe Florey on Easter Sunday, 10 April 1966, only an hour after attending with his family a mass celebrated in Latin by Father Caraman. The funeral mass at nearby Wiveliscombe was also in Latin, as was the special memorial mass on April 21 at Westminster Cathedral in London presided over by Cardinal Heenan. At the end of the memorial service military trumpets sounded throughout the cathedral to honor the army veteran of World War II.

Waugh lies buried on the grounds of Combe Florey, his home for the last decade of his life, where his wife continued to live until her death in June 1973 and where Auberon Waugh and his family now reside. Laura Waugh graciously invited me to visit her there. As we entered the dining room for luncheon she pointed out a bust of her husband, atop which rested Waugh's own officer's dress cap. "This bust is a copy of the original which went with the rest of the contents of his library to the University of Texas," she explained, "but the cap is really my husband's."

After our conversation she went with me to visit the grave. The inscription on the gravestone reads simply: "Evelyn Waugh, Writer." Afterwards I sat in the drawing room in front of the fire with Evelyn Waugh's favorite cat in my lap as I went through the large volume of obituaries which Mrs. Waugh gave me to scan. Of the many tributes paid to Waugh at his death, one of the warmest came from his colleague Graham Greene in the *London Times:*

> Evelyn Waugh was the greatest novelist of my generation, but in the shock of his death, I can only write of my love for him as a friend. . . . We were deeply divided politically, were divided even in our conception of the same church. . . . But Evelyn Waugh had an unshakable loyalty to his friends, even if he may have detested their opinions and sometimes their actions. One could never depend upon him for easy approval or a warm, weak complaisance, but when one felt the need of him he was always there. (15 April 1966)

That loyalty was sometimes reflected in extraordinary and largely unpublicized acts of charity on Waugh's part. In the last months before Ronald Knox died of cancer in August 1957, Douglas Woodruff recalls in his *Tablet* obituary of Waugh, Waugh stayed by his side for several weeks caring for him (19 April 1966). Like Guy Crouchback, Waugh did not let his propensity toward melancholy keep him from extending charity to others. Evidence such as this helps to neutralize the picture of Waugh as the sarcastic and supersophisticated country squire.

So does the anecdote recounted by his old friend Harold Acton about a visit he and Waugh once paid Sinclair Lewis at his home in Florence. By that time the American novelist was a pathetic, used-up man. Lewis told Waugh, "You will have to cross the Atlantic to learn how to write. We are rejuvenating the language. Have *you* added anything new to the English language, Evelyn? Your 'bright young people' are not likely to be remembered. I guess they are already forgotten. But *Main Street* and *Babbit* will always be remembered, so will *Arrowsmith* and *Elmer Gantry*." Waugh sat in charitable silence, although he was extremely irritated.[116] Mrs. Waugh adds that Waugh had always liked "Red" Lewis and thus put up with his remarks even when Lewis was insulting. Waugh was also aware, I am sure, that he did not have to defend his literary output to Sinclair Lewis or anyone else.

I began the Preface of this book with Saul Bellow's observation that "every writer borrows what he needs from himself." The examination of Waugh's fiction which makes up this book demonstrates that a writer borrows from himself in two ways. First, the novelist transmutes the experiences and observations of his personal life into his work; and second, he incorporates into his fiction his personal outlook on life as it develops out of reflection on his experiences. Earlier in this chapter I summed up the role that Waugh's own life and viewpoint played in the creation of his fiction by noting how closely many of his heroes resemble their creator, both in their lives and in their reaction to the modern age. This resemblance holds true from the early heroes such as Tony Last, who, like Waugh, suffered a wrenching marital experience that left him somewhat disenchanted with life, down to the later heroes in whom the identification of author with hero becomes more pronounced, as is the case with Charles Ryder, Guy Crouchback, and Gilbert Pinfold, all of whom emerge from chastening experiences only to withdraw more and more from contact with the modern age.

Were it not for Waugh's private diary and other autobiographical and nonfiction writings, no one would have known just how closely Waugh's life and vision were allied to those of his major characters. One can enjoy Waugh's fiction for its own sake without identifying these parallels between his life and work. Yet the reader who sees the continuity of Waugh's personal experience and philosophy of life with his fiction gains an extra dimension from Waugh's novels. He can savor the world of Evelyn Waugh not merely as the creation of a novelist's imagination but as the re-creation of the era through which he lived: England's Roaring Twenties, the bleak periods bracketing the war, the war years themselves. As Auberon Waugh says in the epigraph of this book, "The world of Evelyn Waugh's novels did, in fact, exist," and because it really existed Waugh the novelist allows his readers to relive with him the decades just past in a way that no historian can. For in Waugh's novels he allows the reader to experience the quality of life in those years.

In summing up the book for the reader in this way I am but recalling the principal purpose of this study: to demonstrate how Waugh's personal life and viewpoint became part of his fiction. In so doing I hope I have been able to deliver that fringe benefit of which I also spoke in the Preface: to increase the reader's appreciation and enjoyment of Evelyn Waugh's fiction.

Throughout his life Waugh hoped to reach that goal at which, he once wrote, all serious artists aim: to leave behind "some objects of permanent value that were not there before him and would not have been there but for him."[117]

Evelyn Waugh got his wish.

Notes

1. Evelyn Waugh, *A Little Learning: The Early Years* (Boston: Little, Brown, 1964), p. 196.

2. Quoted by Jeffrey M. Heath, "A Note on the Waugh Diaries," *Evelyn Waugh Newsletter* 7 (winter 1973): 8.

3. I have drawn my citations from Waugh's diary as it appeared in the *London Observer Magazine* in an eight-part serial (25 March–13 May 1973). Little, Brown plans to publish the diary in book form.

4. Evelyn Waugh, *The Ordeal of Gilbert Pinfold* (Boston: Little, Brown, 1957), p. 4.

5. Evelyn Waugh, *A Little Learning*, p. 27.

6. Evelyn Waugh, "Come Inside," in *The Road to Damascus: The Spiritual Pilgrimage of Fifteen Converts to Catholicism*, ed. John A. O'Brien (New York: Doubleday, 1949), pp. 17–19. This is an excellent summary of the material treated in chapter 6 of *A Little Learning*.

7. Evelyn Waugh, *A Little Learning*, pp. 171, 196, 204.

8. Julian Jebb, "Evelyn Waugh: An Interview," in *Writers at Work*, ed. Alfred Kazin, 3rd ser. (New York: Viking, 1967), p. 108.

9. Evelyn Waugh, "The Curse of the Horse Race," in *Tactical Exercise* (Boston, Little, Brown, 1954), p. 6.

10. Evelyn Waugh, *A Little Learning*, pp. 223, 228.

11. *Ibid.*, pp. 229-30.

12. Harvey Breit, "An Interview with Evelyn Waugh," *New York Times Book Review*, 13 March 1949, p. 23.

13. Jebb, "Evelyn Waugh: An Interview," pp. 109-10.

14. During 1960-67 Chapman and Hall published the Second Uniform Edition of Waugh's fiction (*Helena* is the only novel excluded). For each of the books in this edition Waugh wrote a preface, which I treat together with each book.

15. Evelyn Waugh *A Little Learning*, p. 229.

16. Elaine Bender, "Sour Grapes," *Evelyn Waugh Newsletter* 2 (autumn 1968): 5.

17. This excerpt from Waugh's unpublished essay appears in the *Evelyn Waugh Newsletter* 2 (winter 1972): 8-9.

18. Evelyn Waugh, *Robbery under Law: The Mexican Object Lesson* (American title: *Mexico: An Object Lesson*) (London: Chapman and Hall, 1939), p. 17.

19. Quoted by Paul A. Doyle, *Evelyn Waugh: A Critical Essay* (Grand Rapids: Eerdmans, 1969), p. 16.

20. Jebb, "Evelyn Waugh: An Interview," pp. 108-9.

21. Evelyn Waugh, *Ninety-Two Days* (London: Duckworth, 1934), p. 110.

22. Evelyn Waugh, *Labels: A Mediterranean Journal* (American title: *A Bachelor Abroad*) (London: Duckworth, 1930), pp. 14-15.

23. Evelyn Waugh, *Remote People* (American title: *They Were Still Dancing*) (London: Duckworth, 1931), p. 14.

24. *Ibid.*, p. 57.

25. Evelyn Waugh, *Monsignor Ronald Knox* (Boston: Little, Brown, 1960), p. 243.

26. Quoted by Frederick Stopp, *Evelyn Waugh: Portrait of an Artist* (London: Chapman and Hall, 1958), pp. 32-34. This letter also appears in John Joliffe's essay on Waugh in *Evelyn Waugh and His World*, ed. David Pryce-Jones (Boston: Little, Brown, 1973).

27. Alec Waugh, *My Brother Evelyn and Other Portraits* (New York: Farrar, Straus, and Giroux, 1967), pp. 172-73.

28. Jebb, "Evelyn Waugh: An Interview," p. 108.

29. Alec Waugh, *My Brother Evelyn*, pp. 192–93.

30. Evelyn Waugh, Preface to *When the Going Was Good* (Boston: Little, Brown, 1947), p. ix. This book is a condensation of Waugh's first four travel books.

31. Evelyn Waugh, *Ninety-Two Days*, p. 97.

32. Evelyn Waugh, *Tourist in Africa* (Boston: Little, Brown, 1960), p. 13.

33. Evelyn Waugh, *Waugh in Abyssinia* (London: Longmans, Green, 1936), pp. 49–50.

34. *Ibid.*, p. 118.

35. Alain Blayac, "Technique and Meaning in *Scoop*," *Evelyn Waugh Newsletter* 6 (winter 1972): 6.

36. Alec Waugh, *My Brother Evelyn*, p. 185.

37. William J. Cook, Jr., *Masks, Modes, and Morals: The Art of Evelyn Waugh* (Teaneck, N.J.: Fairleigh Dickinson University Press, 1971), pp. 166–67.

38. Robert Murray Davis, "Evelyn Waugh and Brian Howard," *Evelyn Waugh Newsletter* 4 (autumn 1970): 6.

39. Quoted by Robert Gorham Davis, "Coach into Pumpkin," *New York Times Book Review*, 11 February 1968, p. 1.

40. David Lodge, *Evelyn Waugh* (New York: Columbia University Press, 1971), p. 29.

41. *Basil Seal Rides Again* was published in a limited edition by Little, Brown in 1963, but can also be found in *Esquire*, March 1963.

42. Alec Waugh, *The Early Years* (London: Cassell, 1962), p. 218.

43. Evelyn Waugh, "Come Inside," pp. 18–20.

44. Quoted by Phillips Temple, "Some Sidelights on Evelyn Waugh," *America*, 26 April 1946, p. 76.

45. Eric Linklater, *The Art of Adventure* (London: Macmillan, 1948), p. 49.

46. Christopher Sykes, "Evelyn Waugh the Man," in *Good Talk: An Anthology from BBC Radio*, ed. Derwent May (London: Victor Gollancz, 1968), p. 23. This is a transcription of a BBC

memorial broadcast in which Stirling and other acquaintances of Waugh's participated.

47. Inscription in the bound set of page proofs of the first British edition of *Brideshead Revisited*, which Waugh presented to the library of Loyola College, Baltimore, Maryland, on receiving an honorary degree there 3 December 1947.

48. Evelyn Waugh, personal letter to W. J. Taylor-Whitehead, 17 May 1950, quoted in the *Evelyn Waugh Newsletter* 2 (winter 1968): 3.

49. John Hardy, *Man in the Modern Novel* (Seattle: University of Washington Press, 1964), p. 166.

50. Linklater, *The Art of Adventure,* p. 52.

51. Hardy, *Man in the Modern Novel,* p. 167.

52. Sean O'Faolain, *The Vanishing Hero: Studies of the Hero in the Modern Novel* (New York: Grosset and Dunlap, 1957), p. 38.

53. Thomas C. Ryan, "A Talk with Evelyn Waugh," *Sign* 37 (August 1957): 43.

54. Christopher Hollis, *Evelyn Waugh,* rev. ed. (London: Longmans, Green, 1966), p. 20.

55. Jebb, "Evelyn Waugh: An Interview," pp. 113–14.

56. Quoted by David Lodge, "The Fugitive Art of Letters," in *Evelyn Waugh and His World,* ed. David Pryce-Jones (Boston: Little, Brown, 1973), p. 213.

57. Robert Murray Davis, *"The Loved One:* Text and Context," *Texas Quarterly* (winter 1972): p. 105.

58. Edmund Wilson, *Classics and Commercials: A Literary Chronicle of the Forties* (New York: Farrar, Straus, 1959), pp. 304–5.

59. Ryan, "A Talk with Evelyn Waugh," p. 42.

60. Evelyn Waugh, "American Epoch in the Catholic Church," *Month,* n.s. 2 (November 1949): 300, 308.

61. Terry Southern, *The Journal of the Loved One: The Production Log of a Motion Picture* (New York: Random House, 1965), p. 4.

62. Graham Greene, "The Redemption of Mr. Joyboy," in *The Portable Graham Greene,* ed. Philip Stratford (New York: Viking, 1973), p. 559.

63. Patricia Corr, "Evelyn Waugh: Sanity and Catholicism," in *Evelyn Waugh,* ed. Robert Murray Davis (St. Louis: Herder, 1969), p. 46.

64. Evelyn Waugh, "Work Abandoned," in *The Holy Places* (London: Queen Anne Press, 1952), p. 2.

65. Hollis, *Evelyn Waugh,* p. 29.

66. Quoted by Temple, "Some Sidelights on Evelyn Waugh," p. 76.

67. Evelyn Waugh, "St. Helena, Empress," in *Saints for Now,* ed. Clare Boothe Luce (New York: Sheed and Ward, 1952), pp. 39–43.

68. James F. Carens, *The Satiric Art of Evelyn Waugh* (Seattle: University of Washington Press, 1966), p. 116.

69. Evelyn Waugh, *Robbery under Law,* p. 279.

70. Robert Murray Davis, "On Waugh," in *Modern British Short Novels,* ed. Robert Murray Davis (Glenview, Illinois; Scott, Foresman, 1972), p. 285.

71. Quoted by Temple, "Some Sidelights on Evelyn Waugh," p. 76.

72. Carens, *The Satiric Art of Evelyn Waugh,* p. 152.

73. Doyle, *Evelyn Waugh,* p. 34.

74. Evelyn Waugh, personal letter to Thomas Merton, 27 December 1951, quoted in the *Evelyn Waugh Newsletter* 3 (spring 1969): 4.

75. Jebb, "Evelyn Waugh: An Interview," p. 112.

76. Maryvonne Butcher, "The Ordeal of Gilbert Pinfold," *Dokumente* 13 (December 1957): 7.

77. Jebb, "Evelyn Waugh: An Interview," pp. 112–13.

78. Andrew Rutherford, "Waugh's *Sword of Honor,*" in *Imagined Worlds: Essays on Some English Novels and Novelists,* ed. Maynard Mack and Ian Gregor (London: Metheun, 1968), p. 445.

79. "The Last of Evelyn Waugh," *TLS: Essays and Reviews from the "Times Literary Supplement: 1966"* (London: Oxford University Press, 1967), p. 124.

80. Evelyn Waugh, *Monsignor Ronald Knox,* pp. 110–11.

81. Hubert Van Zeller, O.S.B., "Evelyn Waugh," *Month*, n.s. 36 (July–August 1966): 70.

82. Carens, *The Satiric Art of Evelyn Waugh*, p. 158.

83. Jebb, "Evelyn Waugh: An Interview," p. 112.

84. Evelyn Waugh, *Monsignor Ronald Knox*, p. 85.

85. Malcolm Bradbury, *Evelyn Waugh* (London: Oliver and Boyd, 1964), p. 109.

86. Frederick Stopp, *Evelyn Waugh*, p. 168.

87. Evelyn Waugh, "Sloth," in *The Seven Capital Sins* (New York: William Morrow, 1962), p. 58.

88. Ronald Knox, "The Reader Suspended: Waugh's *Men at Arms*," *Month*, n.s. 8 (October 1952): 237.

89. *Ibid.*, pp. 237–38.

90. Jebb, "Evelyn Waugh: An Interview," p. 112.

91. Rutherford, "Waugh's *Sword of Honor*," pp. 452–53.

92. Evelyn Waugh, personal letter to Dame Edith Sitwell, 9 August 1955, quoted in the *Evelyn Waugh Newsletter* 1 (winter 1967): 4.

93. Quoted by Temple, "Some Sidelights on Waugh," p. 76.

94. Sykes, "Evelyn Waugh the Man," p. 26.

95. Evelyn Waugh, "St. Helena, Empress," pp. 42–43.

96. Jebb, "Evelyn Waugh: An Interview," p. 112.

97. Sykes, "Evelyn Waugh the Man," p. 26.

98. Doyle, *Evelyn Waugh*, p. 37.

99. Evelyn Waugh, "Compassion," *Month*, n.s. 2 (August 1949): 96.

100. Herbert Howarth, "Quelling the Riot: Evelyn Waugh's Progress," in *The Shapeless God: Essays on Modern Fiction*, ed. Harry J. Mooney, Jr., and Thomas F. Staley (Pittsburgh: University of Pittsburgh Press, 1968), pp. 86–87.

101. Quoted by Stopp, *Evelyn Waugh*, p. 46.

102. "The Last of Evelyn Waugh," pp. 123–24.

103. Rutherford, "Waugh's *Sword of Honor*," p. 444.

104. Ryan, "A Talk with Evelyn Waugh," p. 42.

105. James Kirkup, "Evelyn Waugh: Reactionary Rebel," *The Rising Generation* (Tokyo), 1 August 1966, p. 530.

106. Cyril Connolly, "Introduction to *The Loved One*," *Horizon* 17 (February 1948): 76.

107. Bradbury, *Evelyn Waugh*, p. 105.

108. Cf. Frances Donaldson, *Evelyn Waugh: Portrait of a Country Neighbor* (New York: Chilton, 1968), pp. 54*ff.*, for a more detailed account of this incident.

109. Van Zeller, "Evelyn Waugh," p. 71.

110. Rutherford, "Waugh's *Sword of Honor*," p. 460.

111. Evelyn Waugh, *A Little Learning*, p. 1.

112. Van Zeller, "Evelyn Waugh," pp. 69–70.

113. Claud Cockburn, "Evelyn Waugh's Lost Rabbit," *Atlantic Monthly*, 232 (December 1973): 59.

114. Alec Waugh, *My Brother Evelyn*, p. 184.

115. Sykes, "Evelyn Waugh the Man," p. 68.

116. *Ibid.*, p. 33.

117. Evelyn Waugh, *Tourist in Africa*, p. 187.

Selected Bibliography

**Primary Sources: The Works of Evelyn Waugh
(in order of original publication)**

Books

(The original date of publication appears in parentheses after the title of a Waugh work when the edition consulted is of a later date.)

P.R.B.: An Essay on the Pre-Raphaelite Brotherhood: 1847–1854. London: Alastair Graham, 1926.

Rossetti: His Life and Works. London: Duckworth, 1928.

Decline and Fall (1928), with a preface by the author. Second Uniform Edition. London: Chapman and Hall, 1962.

Vile Bodies (1930), with a preface by the author. Second Uniform Edition, rev. London: Chapman and Hall, 1965.

Labels: A Mediterranean Journal (American title: *A Bachelor Abroad*). London: Duckworth, 1930.

Remote People (American title: *They Were Still Dancing*). London: Duckworth, 1931.

Black Mischief (1932), with a preface by the author. Second Uniform Edition, rev. London: Chapman and Hall, 1962.

Ninety-Two Days. London: Duckworth, 1934.

A Handful of Dust (1934) with a preface by the author and an alternative ending. Second Uniform Edition. London: Chapman and Hall, 1964.

Edmund Campion (1935). New York: Doubleday, 1956.

Waugh in Abyssinia. London: Longmans, Green, 1936.

Mr. Loveday's Little Outing and Other Sad Stories. Boston: Little, Brown, 1936.

Scoop (1938), with a preface by the author. Second Uniform Edition, rev. London: Chapman and Hall, 1964.

Robbery under Law: The Mexican Object Lesson (American title: *Mexico: An Object Lesson*). London: Chapman and Hall, 1939.

Put Out More Flags (1942), with a preface by the author. Second Uniform Edition. London: Chapman and Hall, 1966.

Work Suspended: Two Chapters of an Unfinished Novel. London: Chapman and Hall, 1942.

Brideshead Revisited: The Sacred and Profane Memories of Captain Charles Ryder. London: Chapman and Hall, 1945.

When the Going was Good. Boston: Little, Brown, 1946. A condensation of Waugh's first four travel books.

Scott-King's Modern Europe (1947). Boston: Little, Brown, 1949.

Wine in Peace and War. London: Saccone and Speed, 1947.

The Loved One: An Anglo-American Tragedy (1948), with a preface by the author. Second Uniform Edition. London: Chapman and Hall, 1965.

Helena (1950). New York: Doubleday, 1962.

Men at Arms. Boston: Little, Brown, 1952.

The Holy Places. London: Queen Anne Press, 1952.

Love among the Ruins: A Romance of the Near Future. London: Chapman and Hall, 1953.

Tactical Exercise; Boston: Little, Brown, 1954. Contains *Work Suspended, Love among the Ruins* and other short fiction.

Officers and Gentlemen. Boston: Little, Brown, 1955.

The Ordeal of Gilbert Pinfold: A Conversation Piece. Boston: Little, Brown, 1957.

Monsignor Ronald Knox. Boston: Little, Brown, 1960.

Brideshead Revisited: The Sacred and Profane Memories of Captain Charles Ryder, with a preface by the author. Second Uniform Edition, rev. London: Chapman and Hall, 1960.

Tourist in Africa. Boston: Little, Brown, 1960.

Unconditional Surrender (American title: *The End of the Battle*). London: Chapman and Hall, 1961.

Basil Seal Rides Again: The Rake's Regress (1962). Boston: Little, Brown, 1963.

A Little Learning: The Early Years. Boston: Little, Brown, 1964.

Sword of Honor: The Final Version of the Novels: "Men at Arms," "Officers and Gentlemen," and "Unconditional Surrender," with a preface by the author, rev. London: Chapman and Hall, 1965.

The Private Diaries. Edited by Michael Davie. In 8 installments. *London Observer Magazine,* 25 March–13 May 1973.

Articles

"A Commando Raid in Bardia," *Life,* 17 November, 1941; reprinted in *Reader's Digest,* 40 (February 1942): 122–25.

"Fan-fare." *Life,* 8 April, 1946, pp. 53–60.

"The Jesuit Who was Thursday." *Commonweal,* 21 March 1947, pp. 558–61.

"Death in Hollywood." *Life,* 29 September 1947, pp. 73–84.

"Felix Culpa?" *Commonweal,* 16 July 1948, pp. 322–25.

"Come Inside." In *The Road to Damascus: The Spiritual Pilgrimage of Fifteen Converts to Catholicism,* pp. 17–21. Edited by John A. O'Brien. New York: Doubleday, 1949.

Foreword to *Elected Silence* (American title: *The Seven Storey Mountain*), by Thomas Merton. London: Hollis and Carter, 1949; reprinted in *Month,* n.s. 1 (March 1949): 158–59.

"Kicking against the Goad." *Commonweal,* 11 March 1949, pp. 534–36.

"Rossetti Revisited: Pre-Raphaelism and Religion." *Tablet,* 16 July 1949, p. 40.

"Compassion." *Month,* n.s. 2 (August 1949): 79–98.

"American Epoch in the Catholic Church," *Month,* n.s. 2 (November 1949): 293–308.

"The Heart's Own Reasons." *Commonweal,* 17 August 1951, pp. 458–59.

"St. Helena, Empress." In *Saints for Now,* pp. 38–43. Edited by Clare Boothe Luce. New York: Sheed and Ward, 1952.

"Defense of the Holy Places." *Month,* n.s. 7 (March 1952): 135–48.

"Goa: The Home of a Saint." *Month,* n.s. 10 (December 1953): 325–35.

"Scenes from Clerical Life." *Commonweal,* 30 March 1956, pp. 667–68.

"Sloth." In *The Seven Deadly Sins,* pp. 55–64. New York: William Morrow, 1962.

"The Same Again, Please: A Layman's Hopes for the Vatican Council." *National Review,* 4 December 1962, pp. 429–32.

"Oxford Revisited." *Sunday Times* (London), 7 November 1965, p. 53.

Secondary Sources (in alphabetical order by author)

Books

Bradbury, Malcolm. *Evelyn Waugh.* London: Oliver and Boyd, 1964.

Carens, James F. *The Satiric Art of Evelyn Waugh.* Seattle: University of Washington Press, 1966.

Carew, Dudley. *A Fragment of Friendship.* London: Everest, 1975. About Waugh's youth.

Cook, William J., Jr. *Modes, Masks, and Morals: The Art of Evelyn Waugh.* Teaneck, N. J.: Fairleigh Dickinson University Press, 1971.

Davis, Robert Murray, ed. *Evelyn Waugh.* St. Louis: Herder, 1969.

———, Paul A. Doyle, Heinz Kosok, and Charles E. Linck, Jr., eds. *Evelyn Waugh: A Checklist of Primary and Secondary Material.* Troy, N. Y.: Whitston, 1972.

De Vitis, A. A. *Roman Holiday: The Catholic Novels of Evelyn Waugh.* New York: Bookman Associates, 1956.

Donaldson, Frances. *Evelyn Waugh: Portrait of a Country Neighbor.* New York: Chilton, 1968.

Doyle, Paul A. *Evelyn Waugh: A Critical Essay.* Grand Rapids: Eerdmans, 1969.

Greenblatt, Stephen Jay. *Three Modern Satirists: Waugh, Orwell, and Huxley.* New Haven: Yale University Press, 1965.

Hardy, John. *Man in the Modern Novel.* Seattle: University of Washington Press, 1964.

Hollis, Christopher. *Evelyn Waugh.* Rev. ed. London: Longmans, Green, 1966.

Linklater, Eric. *The Art of Adventure.* London: Macmillan, 1948.

Lodge, David, *Evelyn Waugh.* New York: Columbia University Press, 1971.

O'Donnell, Donat [Conor Cruise O'Brien]. *Maria Cross: Imaginative Patterns in a Group of Modern Catholic Writers.* New York: Oxford University Press, 1952.

O'Faolain, Sean. *The Vanishing Hero: Studies of the Hero in the Modern Novel.* New York: Grosset and Dunlap, 1957.

Pryce-Jones, David, ed. *Evelyn Waugh and His World.* Boston: Little, Brown, 1973.

Rolo, Charles, ed. *The World of Evelyn Waugh.* Boston: Little, Brown, 1958.

St. John, John. *To the War with Waugh.* London: Leo Cooper, 1974.

Southern, Terry. *The Journal of the Loved One: The Production Log of a Motion Picture.* New York: Random House, 1965.

Stopp, Frederick J. *Evelyn Waugh: Portrait of an Artist.* London: Chapman and Hall, 1958.

Waugh, Alec. *The Early Years of Alec Waugh.* London: Cassel, 1962.

———. *My Brother Evelyn and Other Portraits.* New York: Farrar, Straus, and Giroux, 1967.

Wilson, Edmund. *Classics and Commercials: A Literary Chronicle of the Forties.* New York: Farrar, Straus, 1950.

Articles

Brady, Charles A. "In Memoriam: Arthur Evelyn St. John Waugh: 1903–1966." *America,* 23 April 1966, pp. 594–95.

Breit, Harvey. "An Interview with Evelyn Waugh." *New York Times Book Review,* 13 March 1949, p. 23.

Butcher, Maryvonne. "Evelyn Waugh, 1903–66." *Dokumente* 22 (1966): 236–38.

————. "The Ordeal of Gilbert Pinfold." *Dokumente* 13 (1957): 6–10.

Cameron, J. M. "Evelyn Waugh, R.I.P." *Commonweal,* 29 April 1966, pp. 167–68.

"Candy in Lotusland: The Film of *The Loved One.*" *Newsweek,* 18 October 1965, pp. 122–27.

Caraman, Philip, S.J. "Evelyn Waugh: A Panegyric." *Tablet,* 30 April 1966, pp. 518–19.

"A Class War." *Time,* 19 January 1962, p. 84.

Cleave, Maureen. "Harriet Waugh: An Interview." *Evening Standard* (London), 17 April 1969, p. 11.

Clinton, Farley. "Days of His Pilgrimage: The Religion of Evelyn Waugh." *Triumph,* April 1967, pp. 31–34.

Cockburn, Claud. "Evelyn Waugh's Lost Rabbit." *Atlantic Monthly* 232 (December 1973): 53–59.

Connolly, Cyril. "Introduction to *The Loved One.*" *Horizon* 17 (February 1948): 76–77.

Crozier, Mary. "Interviewing Mr. Waugh." *Tablet,* 2 July 1960, p. 623.

Davis, Robert Murray. "On Waugh." In *Modern British Short Novels,* edited by Robert Murray Davis, pp. 285–90. Glenview, Illinois: Scott, Foresman, 1972.

————. "*The Loved One:* Text and Context." *Texas Quarterly,* winter 1972, pp. 100–107.

Doyle, Paul A. *"Brideshead* Rewritten." *Catholic Book Reporter,* spring 1962, pp. 9–10.

———. "The Persecution of Evelyn Waugh." *America,* 3 May 1958, pp. 165–69.

"Evelyn Waugh." *New York Times,* 10 April 1966, p. 1.

Evelyn Waugh Newsletter. 1 (1967)–9 (1975).

"Fierce Little Tragedy." *Time,* 7 January 1946, pp. 92–95.

Gardiner, Harold C., S. J. "Waugh's Awry Critics." *America,* 12 January 1946, pp. 409–10.

Grace, William J. "Evelyn Waugh as Social Critic." *Renascence,* 1 (spring 1949): 28–40.

Greene, Graham, "The Redemption of Mr. Joyboy." *Month,* n.s. 2 (January 1949). Reprinted in *The Portable Graham Greene,* edited by Philip Stratford, pp. 557–60. New York: Viking, 1973.

Howarth, Herbert, "Quelling the Riot: Evelyn Waugh's Progress." In *The Shapeless God: Essays on Modern Fiction,* edited by Harry J. Mooney, Jr., and Thomas F. Staley, pp. 67–89. Pittsburgh: University of Pittsburgh Press, 1968.

Jebb, Julian. "Evelyn Waugh: An Interview." In *Writers at Work: The "Paris Review" Interviews,* edited by Alfred Kazin, 3rd ser., pp. 103–14. New York: Viking, 1967.

Kirkup, James. "Evelyn Waugh: Reactionary Rebel." *Rising Generation* (Tokyo), 1 August 1966, pp. 526–31.

Knox, Ronald A. "The Reader Suspended: Waugh's *Men at Arms."* *Month,* n.s. 8 (October 1952): 236–38.

"The Last of Evelyn Waugh." *TLS: Essays and Reviews from the "Times Literary Supplement: 1966."* London: Oxford University Press, 1967, pp. 123–27.

Linck, Charles E., Jr., and Robert Murray Davis. "The Bright Young People in *Vile Bodies." Papers on Language and Literature* 5 (winter 1968): 80–90.

Lunn, Arnold. "Evelyn Waugh Revisited." *National Review,* 27 February 1968, pp. 189–90.

Macaulay, Rose. "Evelyn Waugh: The Best and the Worst."

Horizon 14 (December 1946): 360–76.

Powers, J. F. "Waugh Out West." *Commonweal,* 16 July 1948, pp. 326–27.

Rolo, Charles J. "Evelyn Waugh: The Best and the Worst." *Atlantic* 194 (October 1954): 80–86.

Rutherford, Andrew. "Waugh's *Sword of Honor.*" In *Imagined Worlds: Essays on Some English Novels and Novelists,* edited by Maynard Mack and Ian Gregson, pp. 441–60. London: Metheun, 1968.

Ryan, Thomas C. "A Talk with Evelyn Waugh." *Sign,* 37 (August 1957): 41–43.

St. John, John. "Temporary Officers and Gentlemen." *Sunday Times* (London), 7 September 1969.

"Scribe of the Dark Age." *Time,* 8 April 1946, p. 67.

Staley, Thomas F. "Waugh the Artist." *Commonweal,* 27 May 1966, p. 280.

Sykes, Christopher. "Evelyn Waugh the Man." In *Good Talk: An Anthology from BBC Radio,* edited by Derwent May, pp. 11–34. London: Victor Gollancz, 1968.

The Tablet. 7 January–18 February 1933. Opinions published for and against *Black Mischief.*

Temple, Phillips. "Some Sidelights on Evelyn Waugh." *America,* 27 April 1946, pp. 75–76.

Van Zeller, Hubert, O. S. B. "Evelyn Waugh." *Month.* n.s. 36 (July–August 1966): 69–71.

Vidal, Gore. "The Satiric World of Evelyn Waugh." *New York Times Book Review,* 7 January 1962, p. 1.

Waugh, Auberon. "Waugh's World." *New York Times Magazine,* 7 October 1973, pp. 20–21, 100–102.

West, Stanley. "*Vile Bodies:* A Review." *Saturday Review of Literature,* 5 April 1930, p. 650.

Woodruff, Douglas. "Evelyn Waugh: The Man Behind the Writer." *Tablet,* 16 April 1966, pp. 441–42.

Index

Cameron, J. M., 146
Campion Hall, 52, 125
Camus, Albert, 146
Canterbury, 53
Caraman, Father Philip, S.J.,
122, 149, 155
Cardinal Hinsley, 41
Carens, James, 98, 99, 103,
110
Carroll, Lewis, 20
Catholicism, Roman, x, 2, 14,
17, 22, 24, 29, 40, 51-55,
57, 63, 66, 67-70, 72-74,
87, 94, 99, 108-10, 112,
115, 124, 129, 131-32, 143-
44, 146, 148, 151-52.
Ceylon, 147, 149
Chapman and Hall, 8
Churchill, Randolph, 45, 105
Cockburn, Claud, 153
Coleridge, Samuel Taylor, 36
Combe Florey, 145, 155
Commonweal, 45, 72, 78, 136, 146
Communism, 45, 111, 125, 128,
129, 132, 133
"Compassion," 127, 134, 135
Connolly, Cyril, 147
Cook, William, 43
Cooper, Giles, 140
Cooper, Lady Diana, 35, 154
Coronation Year of Elizabeth
II, 100
Corr, Patricia, 89
Crete, 43, 105, 118-19, 121-
23, 124, 126, 127

Crusades, 111, 154
Crutwell, C.R.M.F., 27
"Curse of the Race Horse,
The," 4

Daily Express, The, 17, 20, 54, 128
Daily Mail, The, 34
Dakar, 105, 117, 127
D'Arcy, Father Martin, S.J.,
xi, 17, 24, 40, 41, 52-54,
60, 66, 73, 97, 122, 149,
151, 152
D'Arms, Teresa, xi, 7, 44, 51,
90, 100, 141, 154
Davie, Michael, xi
Davis, Robert Murray, 46, 83,
100
Day of the Locust, 80
"Death in Hollywood," 81
Debra Lebanos, 23
Decline and Fall, 3, 4, 5, 8-14, 15,
28, 47, 51, 57, 85
Decline and Fall of a Birdwatcher, 13
Deer Park, The, 80
Devasse, Father, 66
Dickens, Charles, 29, 32
Donne, John, 147
Downing Street, 56
Doyle, Paul, 78, 103, 133
Duckworth's, 8, 28
Duggan, Alfred, 66
Duggan, Hubert, 66
Dunne, Philip, 153

Eaton, Dr. Hubert, 82

Index

.5⁰⁰